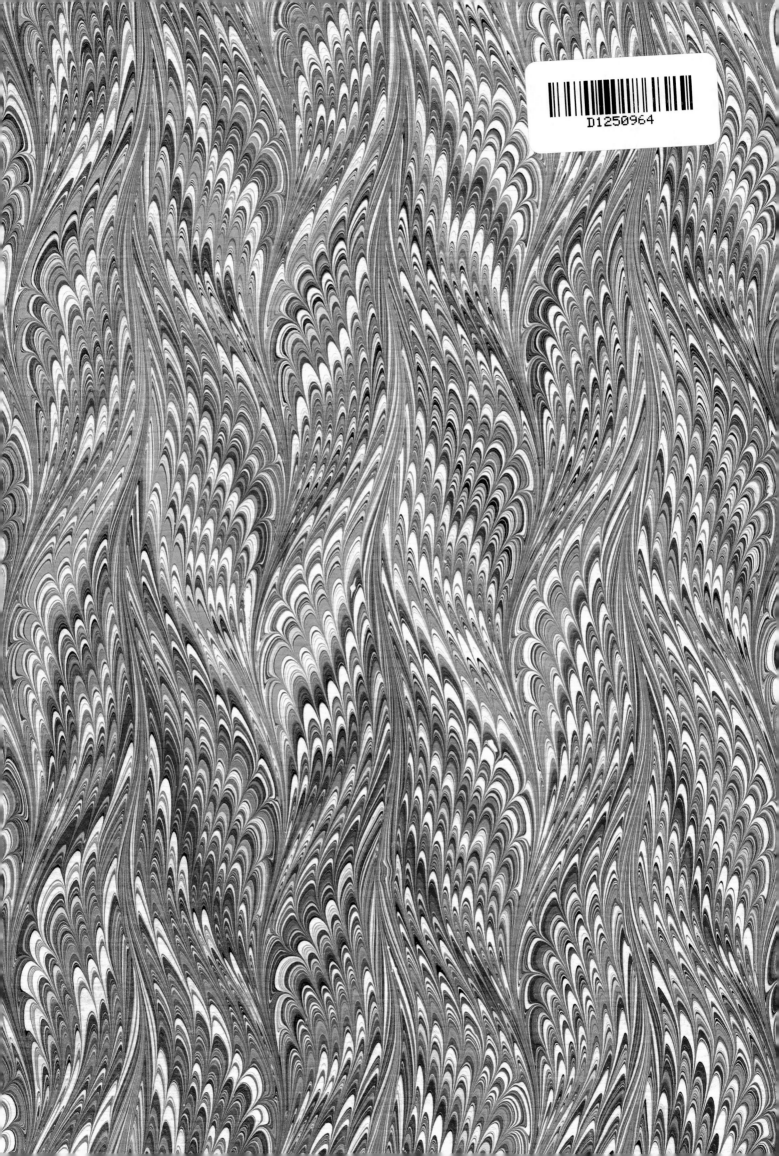

THE BIRDS OF
AMERICA

The Birds of America by John James Audubon was originally issued in 87 sets of five prints, with each set containing one large, one medium and three small plates. This resized edition of Audubon's masterpiece has been created by disbinding one of the two original sets held by the Natural History Museum, London. It includes all 435 images, reproduced as large as possible on the page. In general the small images have been reproduced at approximately ⅔ of the original plate size, the large images at approximately ⅓ and the remainder of the images in between the two sizes. The original numbering and captions have been faithfully recreated, and for this reason there are inconsistencies in the spelling of names and the numbering of plates.

METRO BOOKS
New York
An Imprint of Sterling Publishing
387 Park Avenue South
New York, NY 10016

This 2012 edition published by Metro Books by arrangement with the Natural History Museum, London.

ISBN 978-1-4351-4257-2

For information about custom editions, special sales, and premium and corporate purchases, please contact Sterling Special Sales at 800-805-5489 or specialsales@sterlingpublishing.com.

Manufactured in China

4 6 8 10 9 7 5 3

JOHN JAMES AUDUBON
THE BIRDS OF
AMERICA

METRO BOOKS
New York

Foreword

I N 1804, AT THE AGE OF 19, JOHN JAMES AUDUBON stood in a cave in Pennsylvania looking at a pair of eastern phoebes and had an epiphany: "I looked so intently at their innocent attitudes that a thought struck my mind like a flash of light, that nothing, after all, could ever answer my enthusiastic desires to represent nature, except to copy her in her own way, alive and moving! On I went, forming, literally, hundreds of outlines ... I continued for months together, simply outlining birds as I observed them, either alighted or on the wing".

And so his childhood fascination with drawing birds became his obsession. He wandered the woods and rivers of the wild frontiers of North America shooting, studying, posing, and painting every species of bird he could find, and many years later, the resulting books were to change the worlds of ornithology and natural history art forever.

It is difficult for modern birdwatchers to conceive of the obstacles he must have encountered during those years. Not only the privations of life on the frontier – cold, insects, dirt, hunger – but also the absence of camera and binoculars, and very few other birdwatchers or books as guides. He carried a shotgun and his art supplies, and literally learned about the birds from scratch, by his own observations, simply watching and trying to detect patterns of similarities and differences.

His near total focus on birds led to several business failures, and to hardships for his family, but he (and his equally undaunted wife Lucy) always found a way to get by, and his passion and total commitment shines through in letters and journal entries. Writing about his time in Louisville, Kentucky around 1810, when he was supposed to be helping his business partner run a dry-goods store, he said "I shot, I drew, I looked on Nature only, and my days were happy beyond human conception, and beyond this I really cared not."

Bird illustration before Audubon was primarily stiffly-posed profiles of birds, but the goal that Audubon set for himself at age 19 was to recreate the grace and beauty of the living bird on paper. Still, it took many years for him to break free of tradition and develop this new approach.

The two lower birds in plate 141 – northern goshawk (goshawk) on the left and Cooper's hawk (Stanley hawk) on the right – were painted around 1809, just ten years after his epiphany, and show that he was only adding small embellishments to the traditional stiff and flat poses of the time. Twenty years later, in 1829 just after publication of the finished work began, he painted the much more vibrant and dramatic immature northern goshawk at the top of this plate.

This desire to introduce drama and action to his paintings of birds pushed the boundaries, and straddled the line between science and art. His birds are "very demonstrative, even theatrical and melodramatic at times" wrote John Burroughs in 1902. His critics accused him of sacrificing accuracy for dramatic effect, and there is no doubt that he enjoyed and embellished his stories.

When he painted mockingbirds defending their nest (plate 21), he chose a very dramatic predator – a rattlesnake – rising up out of the branches by the nest. His critics pounced, saying that rattlesnakes do not climb trees. But at the same time the birds are scrupulously accurate, and his portrayal of the aggressive and fearless mockingbirds defending their nest perfectly captures that species' feisty personality.

One of Audubon's artistic tricks was to compress several events into a single composition. His painting of yellow-breasted chats (plate 137), with the female sitting on the nest while three males fly and perch above her, is a very unlikely scenario for this relatively solitary species. The painting makes more sense if we imagine that Audubon wanted us to see several time-lapse images of a single male performing its display flight above the nest and later offering food to the female. It tells a detailed story about the birds as individuals, and it is also ornithologically accurate.

One of the most frenetic paintings in the entire collection (plate 76) is the red-shouldered hawk grappling frantically as a covey of northern bobwhite (Virginian partridge) tumble and scatter in front of it. The hawk's pose appears awkward, but each part of the picture makes sense independently, as if the hawk's left foot was recorded a moment before the right foot, and the right wing a moment before the left. It's a disjointed image, not just a moment, but little bits of many different moments, frozen in time; and it is a very effective record of the explosion of motion and sound that must have accompanied such an event.

It is worth mentioning that one reason the hawk's pose looks awkward to modern viewers is that our perception has been informed by a lifetime of viewing photographic images. Audubon and his contemporaries saw the world only through their own eyes, and fast-moving events like a hawk attacking a covey of quail would have been a blur. Audubon could only imagine the details, which is exactly what he did for this and many other paintings. Presumably he posed the birds as naturally as he could to match the impressions he had accumulated in a lifetime of watching. As an artist he also must have been subconsciously selecting the most elegant and dramatic poses – the most appealing – according to prevailing fashions.

But for all of the drama and violence conveyed in such an image, each individual bird is rendered in exquisitely-crafted detail. They are frozen in time so that, even as they are engaged in the elemental struggle for life or death, Audubon encourages us to admire the beauty of their forms and patterns.

Audubon was very aware of viewers' reactions to his work, and of the need to raise money to continue his work, leading Jonathan Rosen to observe that "Audubon, who was always hustling for subscribers for his grand project, was advertising himself and a romantic version of wild America all at the same time." He consciously wore his hair long, slicked it down with bear grease, and dressed in buckskin frontier garb when he called on English society. This had the desired effect. The English were fascinated by this "American Woodsman" with his tales of life in the wilderness, and his startling paintings of birds. His choice, conscious or not, to illustrate birds in their most dramatic and primeval moments, reflecting a world where nature still reigned supreme, merely reinforced the fascination with his paintings and with him.

It was as if he was saying through his art and his presentation: *These are not your pastoral English country birds, these are birds of the vast unknown American Wilderness, and I have gone into that wilderness, and tamed them and captured them on this paper so you can all enjoy their beauty.* It's no wonder that he found more subscribers in England than in America, and that his work has continued to grow in popularity as the American wilderness recedes into the distant past.

The monumental scope of the work required Audubon's full-time attention for over 12 years. He painted the birds, wrote, oversaw the engraving and the packing of the plates, sold subscriptions in America and Europe, and sometimes even delivered the boxed sets of finished plates to subscribers. In this effort he was helped by his wife, his two sons, and a multitude of friends and assistants who were called upon to do everything from writing and editing text to managing the business to painting vegetation and backgrounds in his plates.

In the end he had painted over 1,050 individual birds (all life-size), in 435 published plates. In addition he co-wrote five volumes of *Ornithological Biographies*, which included his personal observations of the habits of the birds. He travelled from Florida to Labrador to Texas and to the Dakotas, and he crossed the Atlantic eight times.

Recognition for his accomplishment was immediate. Just after its completion in 1839 a Boston newspaper wrote that *The Birds of America* was "unrivalled for the boldness almost amounting to temerity with which it was commenced, the perseverance and untiring zeal with which it was carried on, and the fidelity, industry, and celerity with which it has been completed, will remain an enduring monument to American enterprise and science." It is also a monument to the single-minded determination of one man, and the appeal of the paintings is significantly enhanced by the mythology of that man.

The paintings themselves retain the same appeal today that they must have had to the English in the early 1800s – as a record of an exciting and foreign world that we will never see. Each painting is a snapshot of the American frontier. Of course they are a bit dramatic and over-embellished, but each painting tells a story, not just of the life history of the birds, but also of the excitement and wonder that Audubon experienced as he explored the wilderness. Each one has the power to carry us back to the log cabins and candle-lit parlors, and to the frontier where Audubon found such pleasure in envisioning and recreating the birds' stories. And who doesn't love a good story, well-told?

David Allen Sibley

Drawn by J. J. Audubon. F.R.S.E. F.L.S. M.W.S.

Engraved by W.H.Lizars Edinr.
Retouched by R. Havell Junr. London 1829

Great American Cock Male

Vulgo (Wild Turkey) MELEAGRIS GALLOPAVO

PLATE II.

Yellow-billed Cuckoo

COCCYZUS CAROLINENSIS

Plant Papaw Porcelatriloba

Nº1.

Engraved by W.H.Lizars Edin.
Retouched by R. Havell Junr. London 1829

Drawn by J. J. Audubon F.R.S.E. F.L.S. M.W.S.

PLATE III.

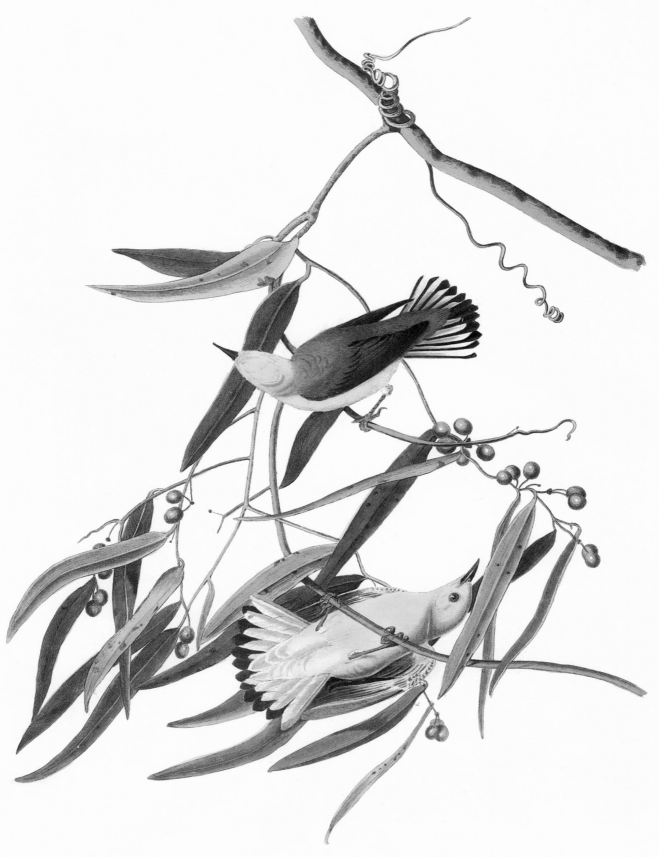

Prothonotary Warbler
DACNIS PROTONOTARIUS
Plant Vulgo Cane Vine

Drawn by J. J. Audubon M.W.S.

Engraved by W. H. Lizars Edinr.

PLATE IV.

Purple Finch
FRINGILLA PURPUREA
Plant Pinus pendula
Vulgo Black Larch

Drawn by J. J. Audubon M.W.S.

Engraved by W. H. Lizars Edinr.

PLATE V.

Bonaparte Fly Catcher

MUSCICAPA BONAPARTII

Plant seed pud Magnolia grandiflora

Drawn by J. J. Audubon M.W.S.

Engraved by W. H. Lizars Edinr.

PLATE VI.

Nº II.

Drawn from Nature by John J. Audubon F.R.S.E. M.W.S.

Engraved by W.H.Lizars Edinr.

Coloured by R. Havell Senr.

Great American Hen & Young.
Vulvo female Wild Turkey MELEAGRIS GALLOPAVO

PLATE VII.

Purple Grackle
QUISCALUS VERSICOLOR.
1. Male 2. Female.
Plant Vulgo, Indian Corn.

Drawn from Nature by John J. Audubon F.R.S.E. F.L.S. M.W.S.   Printed & coloured by R. Havell. Senr.   Engraved by W.H.Lizars Edinr.
Retouched by R. Havell Junr. London 1829

White Throated Sparrow

FRINGILLA PENSYLVANICA

1. Male 2. Female.

Plant Cornus Florida - Vulgo Dog Wood

Drawn from Nature by John J. Audubon F.R.S.E. M.W.S.   Printed & Coloured by R. Havell. Senr.   Engraved by W.H.Lizars Edinr.

PLATE IX.

Selby's Fly Catcher

MUSCICAPA SELBII

Plant Vulgo, Pheasants Eye

Drawn from Nature by John J. Audubon F.R.S.E. M.W.S.   Printed & Coloured by R. Havell. Senr.   Engraved by W.H.Lizars Edinr.

PLATE X.

Brown Lark

ANTHUS AQUATICUS
1.Male. 2.Female.

Drawn from Nature by John J. Audubon F.R.S.E. M.W.S.

Engraved by W.H.Lizars Edinr.

Printed and Coloured by R. Havell Senr.

The Bird of Washington or
Great American Sea Eagle
FALCO WASHINGTONIENSIS Nob.

Drawn from Nature by John J. Audubon F.R.S.E. M.W.S.

Engraved by R. Havell Junr.

Printed and coloured by R. Havell Senr.

PLATE 12.

Baltimore Oriole
ICTERUS BALTIMORE

1 & 2. Males, 3. Female and Nest.

Plant Vulgo, Yellow Poplar
Liriodendron Tulipifera

Drawn from Nature by John J. Audubon F.R.S.E. M.W.S.

Printed & Coloured by R. Havell. Senr.

Engraved by R. Havell Junr.

Snow Bird 1. *Male.* 2. *Female.*

FRINGILLA NIVALIS

Plant Vulgo. Great Swamp Ash

Drawn from Nature by John J. Audubon F.R.S.E. M.W.S.

Printed & Coloured by R. Havell. Senr.

Engraved by R. Havell Junr.

PLATE 14.

Prairie Warbler 1. Male 2. Female.

SYLVIA DISCOLOR

Plant Vulgo. Buffaloe Grass

Drawn from Nature by John J. Audubon F.R.S. M.W.S.   Printed & Coloured by R. Havell. Senr.   Engraved by R. Havell Junr.

PLATE XV.

Blue Yellow back Warbler (1.Male. 2.F.)
SYLVIA AMERICANA
Plant, Vulgo. Louisiana Flag

Drawn by J. J. Audubon F.R.S.E. M.W.S.   Printed & Coloured by R. Havell. Senr.   Engraved by R. Havell Junr.

PLATE 16.

1

2

Engraved, Printed & Coloured by R. Havell & Son, London

Great Footed Hawk Male I. F. 2.

FALCO PEREGRINUS

Drawn from Nature & Published by John J. Audubon F.R.S.E. M.W.S.

Carolina Pigeon or Turtle Dove Male 1. F. 2.

COLUMBA CAROLINENSIS

Plant Steuartia Malacodrendron

Drawn from Nature and Published by John J. Audubon F.R.S.E. M.W.S.

Engraved, Printed & Coloured by R. Havell & Son, London

Bewick's Long Tailed Wren

TROGLODYTES BEWICKII

Plant Vulgo. Iron Wood

Drawn from Nature by John J. Audubon F.R.S.E. M.W.S.

Printed & Coloured by R. Havell. Senr.

Engraved by R. Havell Junr.

PLATE 19.

Louisiana Water Thrush

TURDUS AQUATICUS

Plant Vulgo. Indian Turnip

Drawn from Nature by John J. Audubon F.R.S.E. M.W.S.   Printed & Coloured by R. Havell. Senr.   Engraved by R. Havell Junr.

PLATE 20.

Blue Winged Yellow Warbler Male I. F. 2:
DACNIS SOLITARIA
Plant Vulgo. Wild Althea

Drawn from Nature by John J. Audubon F.R.S.E. M.W.S.   Printed & Coloured by R. Havell. Senr.   Engraved by R. Havell. Junr.

The Mocking Bird 1.Male. 2.F.

TURDUS POLYGLOTTUS

Plant Vulgo. Yellow Jefsamin

Rattlesnake

CROTALUS HORRIDUS

Drawn from Nature & Published by John J. Audubon F.R.S.E. M.W.S.

Engraved, Printed & Coloured by R. Havell & Son, London

Purple Martin 1. Male 2. F.
HIRUNDO PURPUREA
Nest, a Gourd

Drawn from Nature and Published by John J. Audubon F.R.S.E. M.W.S.

Engraved, Printed & Coloured by R. Havell & Son, London

PLATE 23.

Maryland Yellow Throat Male I. F. 2.
SYLVIA TRICHAS
Plant Vulgo—1. Wild Olive—2. Bitter Wood.

Drawn from Nature and Published by John J. Audubon F.R.S.E. M.W.S.

Engraved, Printed & Coloured by R. Havell & Son, London

Roscoe's Yellow Throat
SYLVIA ROSCO
Plant Vulgo. Swamp Oak

Drawn from Nature and Published by John J. Audubon F.R.S.E. M.W.S.

Engraved, Printed & Coloured by R. Havell and Son

Song Sparrow Male 1. F. 2.

FRINGILLA MELODIA

Plant Vulgo. Wortle Berry

Drawn from Nature and Published by John J. Audubon F.R.S.E. M.W.S.

Engraved, Printed & Coloured by R. Havell & Son, London

PLATE 26.

Carolina Parrot Males 1. F. 2. Young 3.

PSITACUS CAROLINENSIS

Plant Vulgo. Cuckle Burr.

Drawn from Nature & Published by John J. Audubon F.R.S.E. M.W.S.

Engraved, Printed & Coloured by R. Havell & Son, London.

PLATE 27.

Red headed Woodpecker Male I. F. 2. Young 3. 4. 5.

PICUS ERYTHROCEPHALUS

Drawn from Nature & Published by John J. Audubon F.R.S.E. M.W.S.

Engraved, Printed & Coloured by R. Havell & Son, London

PLATE 28.

Vireo Solitarius Male.1. F.2.

SOLITARY FLYCATCHER

Plant, Vulgo Cane

Drawn from Nature and Published by John J. Audubon F.R.S.E. M.W.S.

Engraved, Printed & Coloured by R. Havell & Son, London

PLATE 29.

Towee Bunting. Male.1. F.2.
FRINGILLA ERYTHROPTHALMA

Plant, Vulgo, Black-berry

Drawn from Nature and Published by John J. Audubon. F.R.S.E. M.W.S.

Engraved, Printed and Coloured by R. Havell & Son, London.

Vigors Vireo Male
VIREO VIGORSII
Plant, Tradescantia Virginica

Drawn from Nature and Published by John J. Audubon F.R.S.E. M.W.S.

Engraved, Printed & Coloured by R. Havell & Son, London

PLATE 31.

White-headed Eagle. *Male*

FALCO LEUCOCEPHALUS

Fish Vulgo—Yellow mud Cat

Drawn from Nature & Published by John J. Audubon F.R.S.E. F.L.S. M.W.S.

Engraved, Printed & Coloured by R. Havell & Son, London 1828

PLATE 32.

Black-billed Cuckoo
Male 1. F 2.
COCCYZUS ERYTHROPHTHALMUS
Plant. *Magnolia grandiflora*

Engraved, Printed & Coloured by R. Havell & Son. London 1828

Drawn from Nature and Published by
John J. Audubon F.R.S.E. F.L.S. M.W.S.

PLATE 33.

Yellow Bird or American Goldfinch
CARDUELIS AMERICANA
Male 1. F. 2.
Plant, Cnicus lanceolatus, Vulgo Common Thistle

Drawn from Nature and Published by John J. Audubon F.R.S.E. F.L.S. M.W.S.

Engraved, Printed & Coloured by R. Havell & Son, London 1828.

PLATE 34.

Worm-eating Warbler Male I. F. 2.
DACNIS VERMIVORA
Plant Phytolacca decandra. Vulgo, Poke-berry

Drawn from Nature and Published by John J. Audubon. F.R.S.E. F.L.S. M.W.S.

Engraved, Printed & Coloured by R. Havell & Son, London 1828

PLATE 35.

Children's Warbler Male 1. F. 2.
SILVIA CHILDRENI
Plant Cafsia occidentalis. Vulgo Spanish Coffee

Drawn from Nature and Published by John J. Audubon F.R.S.E. F.L.S. M.W.S. Engraved, Printed & Coloured by R. Havell & Son, London 1828

PLATE 36.

Stanley Hawk Male. 1. F. 2.
ASTUR STANLEII

Drawn from Nature & Published by John J. Audubon F.R.S.E. F.L.S. M.W.S.

Engraved, Printed & Coloured by R. Havell & Son. London 1828

PLATE 37.

Gold-winged Woodpecker Male I. F 2.

PICUS AURATUS

Drawn from Nature and Published by John J. Audubon F.R.S.E. F.L.S. M.W.S.

Engraved by Robt. Havell Junr. Printed & Coloured by R. Havell, Senr. London 1828

Kentucky Warbler Male. I. F. 2.
SYLVIA FORMOSA
Plant Magnolia auriculata

Drawn from Nature and Published by John J. Audubon F.R.S.E. F.L.S. M.W.S.

Engraved, Printed & Coloured by R. Havell & Son, London 1828

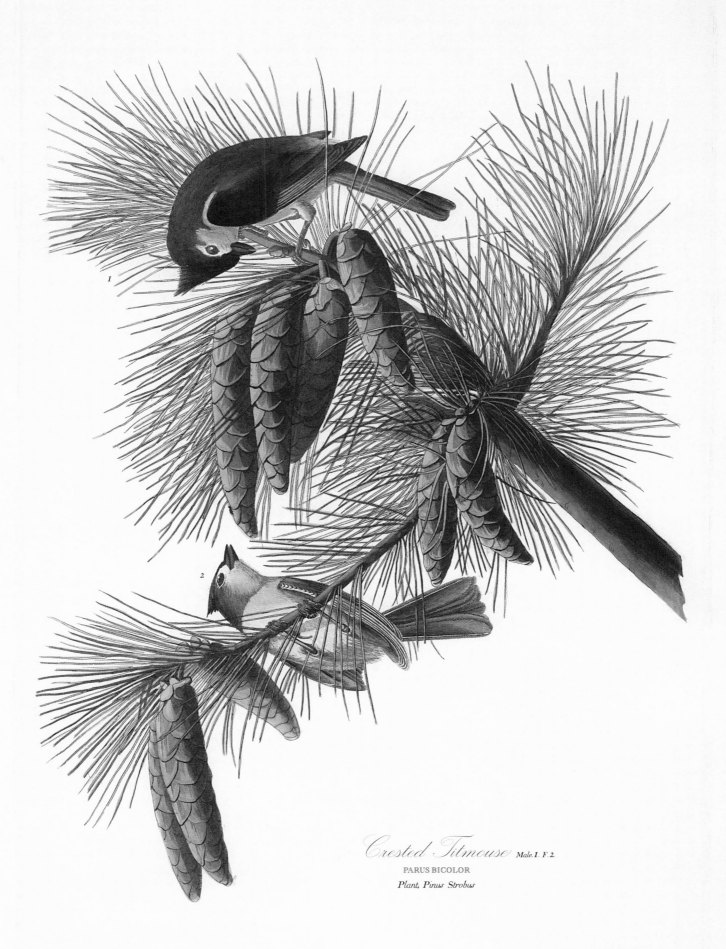

Crested Titmouse Male. 1. F. 2.

PARUS BICOLOR

Plant, Pinus Strobus

Drawn from Nature and Published by John J. Audubon F.R.S.E. F.L.S. M.W.S.

Engraved, Printed & Coloured by R. Havell & Son, London 1828

PLATE 40.

American Redstart Male. 1. F. 2.

MUSCICAPA RUTICILLA

Plant Vulgo, Scrub Elm

Ostrya Virginica

Drawn from Nature and Published by John J. Audubon F.R.S.E. F.L.S. M.W.S.

Engraved by Robt. Havell Junr. Printed & Coloured by R. Havell Senr. London 1828

PLATE 41.

Engraved by R. Havell Junr: Printed & Coloured by R. Havell Senr: London 1828

Ruffed Grouse Male 1 & 2. F. 3

TETRAO UMBELLUS Vulgo. Pheasant

Drawn from Nature & Published by John J. Audubon F.R.S.E. F.L.S. M.W.S.

Orchard Oriole
ICTERUS SPURIUS
Plant Vulgo, honey Locust
Gleditschia triacanthos

Male 1.2. adult.
3 & 4. 2nd and 3rd Year.
5. Female

Drawn from Nature and Published by John J. Audubon F.R.S.E. F.L.S. M.W.S.

Engraved by R. Havell Junr. Printed & Coloured by R. Havell Senr. London 1828

PLATE 43.

Cedar Bird Male. 1. F. 2.

BOMBYCILLA CAROLINENSIS

Plant Vulgo, Red Cedar

Juniper Virginiana

Drawn from Nature and Published by John J. Audubon F.R.S.E. F.L.S. M.W.S.

Engraved by R. Havell Junr. Printed & Coloured by R. Havell Senr. London 1828

PLATE 44.

Summer Red Bird Male old 1. Young 2. F 3.

TANAGRA ÆSTIVA

Plant Vulgo, Wild Muscadine

Vitis rotundifolia

Drawn from Nature & Published by John J. Audubon F.R.S.E. F.L.S. M.W.S.

Engraved by R. Havell Junr. Printed & Coloured by R. Havell Senr. London 1828.

PLATE 45.

Traill's Fly-catcher

MUSCICAPA TRAILLI

Plant Vulgo, Sweet Gum

Liquidamber Styraciflua

Drawn from Nature & Published by John J. Audubon F.R.S.E. F.L.S. M.W.S.

Engraved by R. Havell Junr. Printed & Coloured by R. Havell Senr. London 1828

Barred Owl Male. Adult

STRIX NEBULOSA

Grey Squirrel

Scurius Cinereus

Drawn from Nature & Published by John J. Audubon F.R.S.E. F.L.S. M.W.S.

Engraved by R. Havell Junr. Printed & Coloured by R. Havell. Senr. London 1828.

PLATE 47.

Ruby-throated Humming Bird Male.1. F.2. Young 3.

TROCHILUS COLUBRIS

Plant, Bignania radicans

Vulgo, Trumpet Flower

Drawn from Nature and Published by John J. Audubon F.R.S.E. F.L.S. M.W.S.

Engraved by R. Havell Junr. Printed & Coloured by R. Havell. Senr. London 1828

Cerulean Warbler Male 1. F. 2.

SYLVIA AZUREA

Plant Vulgo. Bear-berry

Ilex Dahon.

Drawn from Nature and Published by John J. Audubon F.R.S.E. F.L.S. M.W.S.

Engraved by R. Havell Junr. Printed & Coloured by R. Havell. Senr. London 1828

Blue-Green Warbler Male
SYLVIA RARA
Plant Vulgo. Spanish Mulberry
Callicarpa Americana.

Drawn from Nature and Published by John J. Audubon F.R.S.E. F.L.S. M.W.S.

Engraved by R. Havell Junr. Printed & Coloured by R. Havell. Senr. London 1828

Swainson's Warbler Male

SYLVICOLA SWAINSONIA

Tree. Vulgo White Oak

Drawn from Nature and Published by John J. Audubon. F.R.S.E. F.L.S. M.W.S.

Engraved by R. Havell Junr. Printed & Coloured by R. Havell. Senr. London 1828

PLATE 51.

Red Tailed Hawk. Male 1. F. 2.
FALCO BOREALIS

Drawn from Nature & Published by John J. Audubon F.R.S.E. F.L.S. M.W.S.

Engraved by R. Havell Junr. Printed & Coloured by R. Havell Senr. London 1829.

Chuck will's widow Male 1. F. 2.

CAPRIMULGUS CAROLINESIS

Plant, Bignonia Capreolata

Drawn from Nature and Published by John J. Audubon F.R.S.E. F.L.S. M.W.S.

Engraved by R. Havell Junr. Printed & Coloured by R. Havell Senr. London 1829

Painted Bunting
FRINGILLA CIRIS
1 & 2. Old Males; 3. M. of 1st. Year; 4. 2nd. Year; 5. Female.
Plant. Prunus Chicasa

Drawn from Nature & Published by John J. Audubon. F.R.S.E. F.L.S. M.W.S.

Engraved by R. Havell Junr. Printed & Coloured by R. Havell Senr. London 1829

PLATE 54.

Rice Bunting. Male 1. F. 2.
ICTERUS AGRIPENNIS
Plant Acer rubrum

Drawn from Nature & Published by John J. Audubon F.R.S.E. F.L.S. M.W.S.

Engraved by R. Havell Junr. Printed & Coloured by R. Havell Senr. London 1829

PLATE 55.

Cuvier's Wren Male
REGULUS CUVIERI
Plant Kalmia Latifolia

Drawn from Nature & Published by John J. Audubon F.R.S.E. F.L.S. M.W.S. Engraved by R. Havell Junr. Printed & Coloured by R. Havell Senr. London 1829

Red-shouldered Hawk
Male I. F. 2.
FALCO LINEATUS

Drawn from Nature & Published by John J. Audubon F.R.S.E. F.L.S. M.W.S.

Engraved by R. Havell Junr. Printed & Coloured by R. Havell Senr. London 1829.

Loggerhead Shrike
LANIUS CAROLINENSIS
Plant Smilax rotundifolia

Drawn from Nature and Published by John J. Audubon F.R.S.E. F.L.S. M.W.S.

Engraved by R. Havell Junr. Printed & Coloured by R. Havell Senr. London–1829.

Hermit Thrush Male 1. F. 2.

TURDUS SOLITARIUS

Drawn from Nature and Published by John J. Audubon F.R.S.E. F.L.S. M.W.S.

Engraved by R. Havell Junr. Printed & Coloured by R. Havell Senr. London 1829

Chesnut Sided Warbler Male 1. F. 2.

SYLVIA ICTEROCEPHALA

Plant Verbascum Blattaria var.
flore albicante
White-flowered Moth Mullein.

Drawn from Nature and Published by John J. Audubon F.R.S.E. F.L.S. M.W.S.

Engraved by R. Havell Junr. Printed & Coloured by R. Havell Senr. London 1829

Carbonated Warbler Male 1. Young 2.

SYLVIA CARBONATA

Plant *Pyrus Botryapium*
Service Tree

Drawn from Nature and Published by John J. Audubon F.R.S.E. F.L.S. M.W.S.

Engraved by R. Havell Junr. Printed & Coloured by R. Havell Senr. London 1829

Great horned-Owl

Male I. F. young 2.
Strix Virginiana

Drawn from Nature & Published by John J. Audubon F.R.S.E. F.L.S. M.W.S.

Engraved by R. Havell Junr. Printed & Coloured by R. Havell Senr. London 1829

PLATE 62.

Passenger Pigeon Male 1. F. 2.
COLUMBA MIGRATORIA

Drawn from Nature & Published by John J. Audubon F.R.S.E. F.L.S. M.W.S.

Engraved by R. Havell Junr. Printed & Coloured by R. Havell Senr. London. 1829.

PLATE 63.

White Eyed Flycatcher Male.
VIREO NOVEBORACENSIS
Plant Melia Azedarach
Vulgo Pride of China

Drawn from Nature & Published by John J. Audubon F.R.S.E. F.L.S. M.W.S.

Engraved by R. Havell Junr. Printed & Coloured by R. Havell Senr. London 1829

Swamp Sparrow Male.

SPIZA PALUSTRIS

Plant Vulgo May Apple
Podophyllum peltatum

Drawn from Nature by Lucy Audubon   Engraved by R. Havell Junr. Printed & Coloured by R. Havell Senr. London 1829

PLATE 65.

Rathbone's Warbler Males.

SYLVIA RATHBONI

Plant Bignonia Capreolata

Drawn from Nature and Published by John J. Audubon F.R.S.E. F.L.S. M.W.S.

Engraved by R. Havell Junr. Printed & Coloured by R. Havell Senr. London 1829

Ivory-billed Woodpecker Male 1. F.2&3.
PICUS PRINCIPALIS

Drawn from Nature & Published by John J. Audubon F.R.S.E. F.L.S. M.W.S.

Engraved by R. Havell Junr. Printed & Coloured by R. Havell Senr. London 1829

PLATE 67.

Red-winged Starling. Adult Male **1**. Young Male **2**. Female Old **3**. Young **4**.
ICTERUS PHŒNICEUS
Plant Acer rubrum
Vulgo Swamp Maple

Drawn from Nature and Published by John J. Audubon F.R.S.E. F.L.S. M.W.S.

Engraved by R. Havell Junr. Printed & Coloured by R. Havell Senr. London-1829.

Republican Cliff Swallow Male 1. F. 2. Egg 3. Nests 4.

HIRUNDO FULVA

Drawn from Nature and Published by John J. Audubon F.R.S.E. F.L.S. M.W.S.

Engraved by R. Havell Junr. Printed & Coloured by R. Havell Senr. London 1829

Bay breasted Warbler Male I. F.2.
SYLVIA CASTANEA
Plant Vulgo, Highland Cotton
Gofsipium herbaceum

Drawn from Nature & Published by John J. Audubon F.R.S.E. F.L.S. M.W.S.

Engraved by R. Havell Junr. Printed & Coloured by R. Havell Senr. London 1829

PLATE 70.

Shape of Tail

Henslow's Bunting

AMMODRAMUS HENSLOWII

1 Spigelia Marilandica
2 Phlox aristata

Drawn from Nature & Published by John J. Audubon F.R.S.E. F.L.S. M.W.S.

Engraved by R. Havell Junr. Printed & Coloured by R. Havell Senr. London 1829

PLATE 71.

Winter Hawk. *Male Adult*

CIRCUS HYEMALIS

Bull Frog

Engraved by R. Havell Junr. Printed & Coloured by R. Havell Senr. London 1829

Drawn from Nature & Published by John J. Audubon F.R.S.E. F.L.S. M.W.S.

PLATE 72.

Swallow-tailed Hawk. Male 1. Female the same.

FALCO FURCATUS

Reptile Vulgo Garter Snake

Engraved by R. Havell Junr Printed & Coloured by R. Havell Senr London. 1829

Drawn from Nature and Published by John J. Audubon F.R.S.E. F.L.S. M.W.S.

PLATE 73.

Wood Thrush Male I. F. 2.

TURDUS MUSTELINUS

Plant Cornus Florida
Vulgo Dog-wood

Drawn from Nature and Published by John J. Audubon. F.R.S.E. F.L.S. M.W.S.

Engraved by R. Havell Junr. Printed & Coloured by R. Havell Senr. London 1829

Indigo-bird Male Adult *1. M. First Year 2. 2nd. 3. F. 4.*
FRINGILLA CYANEA
Plant Schisandra Coccinea
Vulgo Salsparilla

Drawn from Nature and Published by John J. Audubon F.R.S.E. F.L.S. M.W.S.

Engraved by R. Havell Junr. Printed & Coloured by R. Havell Senr. London 1829.

Le petit Caporal
FALCO TEMERARIUS
Male.

Drawn from Nature and Published by John J. Audubon F.R.S.E. F.L.S. M.W.S.

Engraved by R. Havell Junr. Printed & Coloured by R. Havell Senr. London 1829

Virginian Partridge

Male adult 1. Young 2. Female adult 3. Young 4. very young Birds 5.
Perdix Virginiana

Drawn from Nature & Published by John J. Audubon F.R.S. I.&E. F.L.S. &C.

Engraved, Printed & Coloured by R. Havell Junr. 1830

PLATE 77.

Belted Kingfisher Male 1 & 2. F. 3.
ALCEDO ALCYON

Drawn from Nature and Published by John J. Audubon F.R.S. L&E. F.L.S. &C.

Engraved, Printed & Coloured by R. Havell Junr. 1830

Great Carolina Wren Male 1. F. 2.

TROGLODYTES LUDOVICIANUS

Plant Vulgo Dwarf horse Chesnut
Æsculus Pavia

Drawn from Nature and Published by John J. Audubon F.R.S.E. F.L.S. M.W.S.

Engraved, Printed & Coloured by R. Havell Junr. 1830.

Tyrant Flycatcher Male I. F. 2.

MUSCICAPA TYRANNUS

Plant Cotton Wood
Populus candicans

Drawn from Nature and Published by John J. Audubon F.R.S. L&E. F.L.S. &c.

Engraved, Printed & Coloured by R. Havell Junr. 1830

PLATE 80.

Anthus Hypogæus
PHLOX SUBULATA

Engraved, Printed & Coloured by R. Havell Junr 1830

Drawn from Nature and Published by John J. Audubon F.R.S. I&E F.L.S. &C.

Fish Hawk Male.

Vulgo Weak Fish

FALCO HALLÆTUS

Drawn from Nature & Published by John J. Audubon F.R.S. F.L.S. &C.

Engraved, Printed & Coloured by R. Havell Junr. 1830

Caprimulgus vociferus

Whip-poor-will Male I. F. 2. 3.

quercus tinctoria *Vulgo Black Oak.*

Drawn from Nature and Published by John J. Audubon F.R.S. F.L.S. &C.

Engraved, Printed & Coloured by R. Havell Junr. 1830

PLATE 83.

House Wren Male 1. F. 2. Young 3. 4. 5.

TROGLODYTES ÆDON

Drawn from Nature and Published by John J. Audubon F.R.S. F.L.S. &c.

Engraved, Printed & Coloured by R. Havell Junr. 1830.

Blue Grey Flycatcher Male 1. F. 2.
SYLVIA CŒRULA
Plant *Juglans nigra*
Vulgo Black Walnut

Drawn from Nature and Published by John J. Audubon F.R.S. F.L.S. &C.

Engraved, Printed & Coloured by R. Havell Junr. 1830

Yellow Throat Warbler Male.
SYLVIA PENSILIS.
Plant Castanea pumila
Vulgo Chink-apin

Drawn from Nature & Published by John J. Audubon F.R.S. F.L.S. &c.

Engraved, Printed & Coloured by R. Havell Junr. 1830

Black Warrior Male 1. F. 2.

FALCO HARLANI

Drawn from Nature & Published by John J. Audubon F.R.S's. L&E. F.L.S. &C.

Engraved, Printed & Coloured by R. Havell Junr. London 1830

Florida Jay. Male 1. F. 2.
GARRULUS FLORIDANUS

Diospyros Virginiana
Vulgo Persimon

Drawn from Nature and Published by John J. Audubon F.R.S.'s. L&E. F.L.S. &C.

Engraved, Printed & Coloured by R. Havell Junr. London 1830.

Autumnal Warbler Male 1. F. 2.

SYLVIA AUTUMNALIS

Plant Betula papyrifera
Vulgo Canœ Birch

Drawn from Nature and Published by John J. Audubon F.R.S's. L&E. F.L.S. &C.

Engraved, Printed & Coloured by R. Havell Junr. London 1830

Nashville Warbler Male 1. F. 2.

SYLVIA RUBRICAPILLA

Plant Ilex
Vulgo Spice Wood

Drawn from Nature and Published by John J. Audubon F.R.S.'s. L&E. F.L.S. &C.

Engraved, Printed & Coloured by R. Havell Junr. London 1830.

PLATE 90.

Black and white Creeper

SYLVIA VARIA

Pinus pendula
Vulgo Black Larch

Drawn from Nature and Published by John J. Audubon F.R.S's. L&E. F.L.S. &C.

Engraved, Printed & Coloured by R. Havell Junr. London 1830

PLATE 91.

Broad-winged Hawk Male 1. F. 2.

FALCO PENNSYLVANICUS

Plant Juglans porcina
Vulgo Pig-nut

Drawn from Nature & Published by John J. Audubon F.R.S.'s. L&E. F.L.S.&C.

Engraved, Printed & Coloured by R. Havell Junr. London 1830

PLATE 92.

Pigeon Hawk Male 1. F. 2.
FALCO COLUMBARIUS

Drawn from Nature and Published by John J. Audubon F.R.S.'s. L&E. F.L.S.&C.

Engraved, Printed & Coloured by R. Havell Junr. London-1830.

PLATE 93.

Sea-side Finch Male 1. F.2.
FRINGILLA MARITIMA
Plant Rosa Carolina
Vulgo Wild Rose

Drawn from Nature and Published by John J. Audubon F.R.S.'s. L&E. F.L.S. &C.

Engraved, Printed & Coloured by R. Havell Junr. London 1830.

Bay-winged Bunting. Male.

FRINGILLA GRAMINEA

Drawn from Nature and Published by John J. Audubon F.R.S.'s. L&E. F.L.S. &C.

Plant Cactus opuntia
Vulgo Prickly Pear

Engraved, Printed & Coloured by R. Havell Junr. London 1830

PLATE 95.

Blue-eyed yellow Warbler
SYLVIA ÆSTIVA
Plant Wisterea

Drawn from Nature and Published by John J. Audubon F.R.S's. L&E. F.I.S. &C.

Engraved, Printed & Coloured by R. Havell Junr. London 1830

Columbia Jay Male I. F. 2.
GARRULUS ULTRAMARINUS

Drawn from Nature & Published by John J. Audubon F.R.S's. L&E. F.L.S. &C.

Engraved, Printed & Coloured by R. Havell Junr. London 1830

PLATE 97.

Mottled Owl Adult 1. Young 2 & 3.
STRIX ASIO
Plant Pinus inops
Vulgo Jersey Pine

Drawn from Nature and Published by John J. Audubon F.R.S's. L&E. F.L.S. &C.

Engraved, Printed & Coloured by R. Havell Junr. London 1830

Marsh Wren Male 1. F 2 & 3. Nest 4.
TROGLODYTES PALUSTRIS

Drawn from Nature and Published by John J. Audubon F.R.S.'s. L&E. F.L.S. &c.　　　　　　　　Engraved, Printed & Coloured by R. Havell Junr. London 1830.

PLATE 99.

Nº 20.

Cow Bunting Male 1. F. 2.

ICTERUS PECORIS

Engraved, Printed & Coloured by R. Havell Junr London 1830

Drawn from Nature and Published by John J. Audubon FRS's L&E FLS &C.

Green-blue, or White, Bellied Swallow. Male 1. F.2.
HIRUNDO BICOLOR

Drawn from Nature and Published by John J. Audubon F.R.S.'s. L&E. F.L.S. &C.

Engraved, Printed & Coloured by R. Havell Junr. London 1830

PLATE CI.

Raven

CORVUS CORAX

Male.

Thick Shell-bark Hickory. Juglans laciniosa

Drawn from Nature by J. J. Audubon F.R.S. F.L.S.

Engraved, printed & Coloured by R. Havell, Junr.

PLATE CII.

Blue Jay

CORVUS CRISTATUS

Male. 1. Female. 2. 3.

Drawn from Nature by J. J. Audubon F.R.S. F.L.S.

Engraved, printed & Coloured by R. Havell, Junr.

Canada Warbler
SYLVIA PARDALINA
Male. 1. Female. 2.
Big Laurel. Rhododendron Maximum.

Drawn from Nature by J. J. Audubon F.R.S. F.L.S.

Engraved, printed & Coloured by R. Havell, Junr.

Chipping Sparrow
FRINGILLA SOCIALIS
Male.
Black Locust. Robinia Pseudacacia.

Drawn from Nature by J. J. Audubon F.R.S. F.L.S.

Engraved, printed & Coloured by R. Havell, Junr.

Red-breasted Nuthatch
SITTA CANADENSIS
Male. 1. Female. 2.

Drawn from Nature by J. J. Audubon F.R.S. F.L.S.

Engraved, printed & Coloured by R. Havell, Junr.

Black Vulture or Carrion Crow Male 1 and Female 2. CATHARTES ATRATUS. American Deer. Cervus virginianus

Engraved, Printed & Coloured by R. Havell London 1831

Canada Jay
CORVUS CANADENSIS, Linn.
Male 1. Female 2.
White Oak. Quercus alba.

Drawn from Nature by J. J. Audubon F.R.S. F.L.S.

Engraved, Printed & Coloured by R. Havell, London 1831.

Fox-coloured Sparrow
FRINGILLA ILIACA
Male 1. Female 2.

Drawn from Nature by J. J. Audubon FRS. FLS.

Engraved, Printed & Coloured by R. Havell, London 1854

PLATE CIX.

Savannah Finch FRINGILLA SAVANNA *Male 1. Female 2. 1 Spigelia Marilandica. 2 Phlox aristata.*

Drawn from Nature by J. J. Audubon F.R.S. F.L.S.   Engraved, Printed & Coloured by R. Havell, London 1831.

Hooded Warbler

SYLVIA MITRATA

Male 1. Female 2.

Drawn from Nature by J. J. Audubon F.R.S. F.L.S.

Engraved, Printed & Coloured by R. Havell, London 1831

PLATE CXI.

Pileated Woodpecker

PICUS PILEATUS. Linn

Adult Male, 1. Adult Female, 2. Young Males, 3, 4
Racoon Grape. Vitis æstivalis

Drawn from Nature by J. J. Audubon F.R.S. F.L.S.

Engraved, Printed & Coloured by R. Havell.

PLATE CXII.

Downy Woodpecker
PICUS PUBESCENS
Male, I. Female, 2.
Bignonia capreolata

Drawn from Nature by J. J. Audubon F.R.S. F.L.S.

Engraved, Printed & Coloured by R. Havell. London. 1831.

Blue-bird

SYLVIA SIALIS
Male 1. Female 2. Young 3.
Great Mullein Verbascum Thapsus

Drawn from Nature by J. J. Audubon F.R.S. F.L.S.

Engraved, Printed & Coloured by R. Havell. London. 1831.

White-crowned Sparrow
FRINGILLA LEUCOPHRYS
Male 1. Female 2.
Summer Grape. Vitis Æstivalis.

Drawn from Nature by J. J. Audubon F.R.S. F.L.S.

Engraved, Printed & Coloured by R. Havell. London 1831

PLATE CXV.

Wood Pewee MUSCICAPA VIRENs, *Male.* Swamp Honeysuckle. AZalea biscosa.

Drawn from Nature by J. J. Audubon F.R.S. F.L.S.

Engraved, Printed & Coloured by R. Havell. London 1831.

PLATE CXVI.

Ferruginous Thrush
TURDUS RUFUS. Linn
Male, 1. Female, 2.
Black-jack Oak, Quercus nigra
Black Snake

Drawn from Nature by J. J. Audubon F.R.S. F.L.S.   Engraved, Printed & Coloured by R. Havell, London

Missississippi Kite,

FALCO PLUMBEUS. Gmel.
Male, 1. Female, 2.

Drawn from Nature by J. J. Audubon F.R.S. F.L.S.

Engraved, Printed & Coloured by R. Havell.

Warbling Flycatcher,

MUSCICAPA GILVA. Vieill,

Male, 1. Female, 2.

Swamp Magnolia Magnolia Glauca.

Drawn from Nature by J. J. Audubon F.R.S. F.L.S.

Engraved, Printed & Coloured by R. Havell.

Yellow-throated Vireo,

VIREO FLAVIFRONS. Vieill,
Male.
Swamp Snow-ball. Hydrangea quercifolia.

Drawn from Nature by J. J. Audubon F.R.S. F.L.S.

Engraved, Printed & Coloured by R. Havell, London.

PLATE CXX.

Pewit Flycatcher
MUSCICAPA FUSCA. Gmel,
Male, 1. Female, 2.
Cotton plant Gossypium

Drawn from Nature by J. J. Audubon F.R.S. F.L.S.

Engraved, Printed & Coloured by R. Havell.

PLATE CXXI.

Drawn from Nature by J. J. Audubon F.R.S. F.L.S.   *Snowy Owl* STRIX NYCTEA. Linn *Male, 1. Female, 2.*   Engraved, Printed & Coloured by R. Havell, London

PLATE CXXII.

Blue Grosbeak, FRINGILLA CORULEA. Bonap *Male, 1. Female, 2. Young, 3. Dog-wood Cornus florida.*

Drawn from Nature by J. J. Audubon F.R.S. F.L.S.

Engraved, Printed & Coloured by R. Havell, London

PLATE CXXIII.

Black & Yellow Warbler, SYLVIA MACULOSA. Lath. *Male, 1. Female, 2. Flowering Rasp-berry. Rubus odoratus.*

Drawn from Nature by J. J. Audubon. F.R.S. F.L.S.

Engraved, Printed & Coloured by R. Havell, London.

PLATE CXXIV.

Green Black-capt Flycatcher, MUSCICAPA PUSILLA. Wils. *Male,* 1. *Female,* 2. *Snakes-head. Chelone glabra.*

Drawn from Nature by J. J. Audubon F.R.S. F.L.S.

Engraved, Printed & Coloured by R. Havell, London.

PLATE CXXV.

Brown-headed Nuthatch, SITTA PUSILLA. Lath, *Male, 1. Female, 2.*

Drawn from Nature by J. J. Audubon F.R.S. F.L.S.

Engraved, Printed & Coloured by R. Havell, London.

White-headed Eagle

FALCO LEUCOCEPHALUS. Linn

Young.

Drawn from Nature by J. J. Audubon F.R.S. F.L.S.

Engraved, Printed & Coloured by R. Havell, London

PLATE CXXVII.

Rose-breasted Grosbeak, FRINGILLA LUDOVICIANA. Bonap, *Male,* 1. *Female,* 2. *Young in autumn,* 3. *Young,* 4. *Ground Hemlock, Taxus canadensis.*

Drawn from Nature by J. J. Audubon F.R.S. F.L.S.

Engraved, Printed & Coloured by R. Havell, London

PLATE CXXVIII.

Cat Bird.
TURDUS FELIVOX. Vieill
Male, I. Female, 2.
Black-berry. Rubus villosus.

Drawn from Nature by J. J. Audubon F.R.S. F.L.S.

Engraved, Printed & Coloured by R. Havell, London.

PLATE CXXIX.

Great Crested Flycatcher,

MUSCICAPA CRINITA. Linn,

Male.

Drawn from Nature by J. J. Audubon F.R.S. F.L.S.

Engraved, Printed & Coloured by R. Havell.

PLATE CXXX.

Yellow-winged Sparrow,

FRINGILLA PASSERINA. Wils *Male. Phlox subulata.*

Drawn from Nature by J. J. Audubon F.R.S. F.L.S.

Engraved, Printed & Coloured by R. Havell, London

PLATE CXXXI.

American Robin

TURDUS MIGRATORIUS

Male, 1. Female, 2. Young, 3.

Chestnut oak. Quercus Prinus

Drawn from Nature by J. J. Audubon F.R.S. F.L.S.

Engraved, Printed & Coloured by R. Havell, London 1832.

PLATE CXXXII.

Three-toed Woodpecker, PICUS TRIDACTYLUS. Linn *Males, 1. Female, 2.*

Drawn from Nature by J. J. Audubon F.R.S. F.L.S.

Engraved, Printed & Coloured by R. Havell, London 1832

Black-poll Warbler,

SYLVIA STRIATA. Lath,
Male, 1. Female, 2.
Black Gum Tree. Nyssa aquatica.

Drawn from Nature by J. J. Audubon F.R.S. F.L.S.

Engraved, Printed & Coloured by R. Havell, London 1832

PLATE CXXXIV.

Hemlock Warbler,

SYLVIA PARUS. Wils.
Male, 1. Female, 2.
Dwarf Maple. Acer spicatum.

Drawn from Nature by J. J. Audubon F.R.S. F.L.S.

Engraved, Printed & Coloured by R. Havell, London 1832.

PLATE CXXXV.

Blackburnian Warbler,
SYLVIA BLACKBURNIA. Lath.
Male.
Phlox maculata.

Drawn from Nature by J. J. Audubon F.R.S. F.L.S.

Engraved, Printed & Coloured by R. Havell, London 1832

Meadow Lark. STURNUS LUDOVICIANUS, Linn *Males,1. Females,2. Gerardia flava*

Drawn from Nature by J. J. Audubon F.R.S. F.L.S.

Engraved, Printed & Coloured by R. Havell. London 1832.

Yellow-breasted Chat, ICTERIA VIRIDIS. Bonap, *Males,1. Female,2. Sweet Briar Rosa rubiginosa.*

Drawn from Nature by J. J. Audubon F.R.S. F.L.S.

Engraved, Printed & Coloured by R. Havell, London 1832.

Connecticut Warbler,

SYLVIA AGILIS. Wils,
Male, I. Female, 2.

Gentiana saponaria.

Drawn from Nature by J. J. Audubon F.R.S. F.L.S.   Engraved, Printed & Coloured by R. Havell. London 1832.

PLATE CXXXIX.

Field Sparrow FRINGILLA PUSILLA. Wils,

Drawn from Nature by J. J. Audubon F.R.S. F.L.S.

Male. Calopogon pulchellum, & Vaccinium tenellum,

Engraved, Printed & Coloured by R. Havell, London 1832

Pine Creeping Warbler,

SYLVIA PINUS. Lath *Male, I. Female, 2. Yellow Pine*

Drawn from Nature by J. J. Audubon F.R.S. F.L.S.

Engraved, Printed & Coloured by R. Havell, London 1831.

PLATE CXLI.

Goshawk

FALCO PALUMBARIUS. Linn

Adult Male,1. Young, 2.

Stanley Hawk

FALCO STANLEII. Aud

Adult, 3.

Drawn from Nature by J. J. Audubon F.R.S. F.L.S.

Engraved, Printed & Coloured by R. Havell, London

PLATE CXLII.

American Sparrow Hawk, FALCO SPARVERIUS. Linn *Male,* I. *Female,* 2. *Butter-nut or White walnut Juglans cinerea*

Drawn from Nature by J. J. Audubon F.R.S. F.L.S.

Engraved, Printed & Coloured by R. Havell, London.

PLATE CXLIII.

Golden-crowned Thrush,

Drawn from Nature by J. J. Audubon F.R.S. F.L.S.   TURDUS AUROCAPILLUS. Wils *Male 1 Female 2 Woody Nightshade. Solanum Dulcamara.*   Engraved, Printed & Coloured by R. Havell, London 1832.

PLATE CXLIV.

Small Green Crested Flycatcher,
MUSCICAPA ACADICA. Gmel,
Male, 1. *Female,* 2.
Sassafras. Laurus Sassafras

Drawn from Nature by J. J. Audubon F.R.S. F.L.S.

Engraved, Printed & Coloured by R. Havell, London 1832.

Yellow Red-poll Warbler,

SYLVIA PETECHIA. Lath
Male, I. *Female,* 2.
Helenium quadridentatum

Drawn from Nature by J. J. Audubon F.R.S. F.L.S.

Engraved, Printed & Coloured by R. Havell, London 1832

Fish Crow
CORVUS OSSIFRAGUS, Wils
Male, I. Female, 2.
Vulgo Honey-Locust. Gleditschia Hiacanthos

Drawn from Nature by J. J. Audubon F.R.S. F.L.S.

Engraved, Printed & Coloured by R. Havell, London 1832.

PLATE CXLVII.

Night Hawk,
CAPRIMULGUS VIRGINIANUS. Brifs
Male, 1. Female, 2.
White Oak. Quercus alba.

Drawn from Nature by J. J. Audubon F.R.S. F.L.S.

Engraved, Printed & Coloured by R. Havell, London 1832

PLATE CXLVIII.

Pine Swamp Warbler,
SYLVIA SPHAGNOSA. Bonap
Male, 1. Female, 2.
Hobble Bush. Vibernum lantanoides.

Drawn from Nature by J. J. Audubon F.R.S. F.L.S.

Engraved, Printed & Coloured by R. Havell, London 1832

PLATE CXLIX.

Sharp-tailed Finch,

FRINGILLA CAUDACUTA. Wils.

Male I. Female. 2.

Drawn from Nature by J. J. Audubon F.R.S. F.L.S.

Engraved, Printed & Coloured by R. Havell, London 1832.

PLATE CL.

Red-eyed Vireo

VIREO OLIVACEUS. Bonap.
Male.
Honey Locust Gleditschia hiacanthos

Drawn from Nature by J. J. Audubon F.R.S. F.L.S.

Engraved, Printed & Coloured by R. Havell, London 1832.

Turkey Buzzard
CATHARTES ATRATUS
Male, 1. Young, 2.

Drawn from Nature by J. J. Audubon F.R.S. F.L.S.

Engraved, Printed & Coloured by R. Havell, London 1832

PLATE CLII.

White-breasted Black-capped Nuthatch

Drawn from Nature by J. J. Audubon F.R.S. F.L.S.

SITTA CAROLINENSIS. Brifs *Male, 1. Female, 2.*

Engraved, Printed & Coloured by R. Havell, London 1832.

Yellow-crown Warbler,

SYLVIA CORONATA. Lath
Male, I. Young, 2.
Iris versicolor.

Drawn from Nature by J. J. Audubon F.R.S. F.L.S.

Engraved, Printed & Coloured by R. Havell, London 1832.

PLATE CLIV.

Tennessee Warbler

SYLVIA PEREGRINA. Wils
Male
Prunus. sp.

Drawn from Nature by J. J. Audubon F.R.S. F.L.S.

Engraved, Printed & Coloured by R. Havell, London 1832.

Black-throated Blue Warbler,
SYLVIA CANADENSIS. LATH
Male.
Canadian Columbine. Aquilegia canadensis.

Drawn from Nature by J. J. Audubon F.R.S. F.L.S.

Engraved, Printed & Coloured by R. Havell, London 1832.

PLATE CLVI.

American Crow

CORVUS AMERICANUS
Male.
Black Walnut, Corvus americanus
Nest of the Ruby-throated Humming Bird.

Drawn from Nature by J. J. Audubon F.R.S. F.L.S.

Engraved, Printed & Coloured by R. Havell, London

PLATE CLVII.

Rusty Grakle,
QUISCALUS FERRUGINEUS. Bonap
Male, 1. Female, 2. Young, 3.
Black Haw

Drawn from Nature by J. J. Audubon F.R.S. F.L.S.

Engraved, Printed & Coloured by R. Havell, London 1835

American Swift,
CYPSELUS PELASGIUS. Temm
Male, 1. Female, 2.
Nests.

Drawn from Nature by J. J. Audubon E.R.S. F.L.S.

Engraved, Printed & Coloured by R. Havell, London 1833

Cardinal Grosbeak,
FRINGILLA CARDINALIS. Bonap
Male, 1. Female, 2.
Wild Almond.

Drawn from Nature by J. J. Audubon F.R.S. F.L.S.

Engraved, Printed & Coloured by R. Havell, London 1833.

Black-capped Titmouse
PARUS ATRICAPILLUS. Linn,
Male, 1. Female, 2.
Supple-jack

Drawn from Nature by J. J. Audubon F.R.S. F.L.S.

Engraved, Printed & Coloured by R. Havell, London 1833

Brasilian Caracara Eagle

POLYBORUS VULGARIS

Drawn from Nature by J. J. Audubon F.R.S. F.L.S.

Engraved, Printed & Coloured by R. Havell, London 1833.

PLATE CLXII.

Zenaida dove
COLUMBA ZENAIDA
Male, 1. Female, 2.
Anona

Drawn from Nature by J. J. Audubon F.R.S. F.L.S.

Engraved, Printed & Coloured by R. Havell, London 1833

PLATE CLXIII.

Palm Warbler

SYLVIA PALMARUM.
Male, 1. Young, 2.
Wild Orange.

Drawn from Nature by J. J. Audubon F.R.S. F.L.S.

Engraved, Printed & Coloured by R. Havell, London 1833.

PLATE CLXIV.

Tawny Thrush

TURDUS WILSONII. *Male, Habenaria Lacera – Cornus Canadensis*

Drawn from Nature by J. J. Audubon F.R.S. F.L.S.

Engraved, Printed & Coloured by R. Havell, London 1833.

PLATE CLXV.

Bachmans Finch
FRINGILLA BACHMANI.
Male,
Pinckneya Pubens

Drawn from Nature by J. J. Audubon F.R.S. F.L.S.

Engraved, Printed & Coloured by R. Havell, London 1833

Rough-legged Falcon
FLACO LAGOPUS
Male.

Drawn from Nature by J. J. Audubon F.R.S. F.L.S.

Engraved, Printed & Coloured by R. Havell, London 1833.

PLATE CLXVI.

Key-west Dove. COLUMBA MONTANA.
Male. 1. Female. 2.

Drawn from Nature by J. J. Audubon F.R.S. F.L.S.

Engraved, Printed & Coloured by R. Havell. London 1833.

PLATE CLXVIII.

Forked-tailed Flycatcher MUSCICAPA SAVANA *Male. Gordonia Lasianthus*

Drawn from Nature by J. J. Audubon F.R.S. F.L.S.

Engraved, Printed & Coloured by R. Havell, London 1833.

PLATE CLXIX.

Drawn from Nature by J. J. Audubon F.R.S. F.L.S.

Mangrove Cuckoo COCCYZUS SENICULUS. *Male.*

Engraved, Printed & Coloured by R. Havell, 1833.

Gray Tyrant
TYRANNUS GRISENS

Agati grandiflora

Drawn from Nature by J. J. Audubon F.R.S. F.L.S.

Engraved, Printed & Coloured by R. Havell, 1833.

Barn Owl
STRIX FLAMMEA
Male, 1. Female, 2.
Ground Squirrel, Sciurus Shiatus

Drawn from Nature by J. J. Audubon F.R.S. F.L.S.   Engraved, Printed & Coloured by R. Havell, 1833.

PLATE CLXXII.

Drawn from Nature by J. J. Audubon F.R.S. F.L.S.

Blue-headed Pigeon
COLUMBA CYANOCEPHALA
Male.1. Female.2.

Engraved, Printed & Coloured by R. Havell 1833.

Barn Swallow,

HIRUNDO AMERICANA.
Male, 1. Female, 2.

Drawn from Nature by J. J. Audubon F.R.S. F.L.S.

Engraved, Printed & Coloured by R. Havell, 1833.

Olive sided Flycatcher,
MUSCICAPA INORNATA.
Male, 1. Female, 2.
Pinus Balsamea. Fir Balsam.

Drawn from Nature by J. J. Audubon F.R.S. F.L.S.

Engraved, Printed & Coloured by R. Havell, London 1835.

PLATE CLXXV.

Nuttalls lesser-marsh Wren,

TROGLODITES BREVIROSTRIS.

Male, I. Female, 2.

Drawn from Nature by J. J. Audubon F.R.S. F.L.S.

Engraved, Printed & Coloured by R. Havell, 1833.

PLATE CLXXVI.

Spotted Grous

TETRAO CANADENSIS

Males.1. Females.2.

3 Trillium pictum, 4 Streptopus distortus

Drawn from Nature by J. J. Audubon F.R.S. F.L.S.

Engraved, Printed & Coloured by R. Havell. London 1833.

PLATE CLXXVII.

White-crowned Pigeon
COLUMBA LEUCOCEPHALA
Male. 1. Female. 2.
Cordia Sebestena

Drawn from Nature by J. J. Audubon F.R.S. F.L.S.

Engraved, Printed & Coloured by R. Havell, London 1833.

Orange-crowned Warbler, SYLVIA CELATA *Male.1. Female.2. Vaccinium*

Drawn from Nature by J. J. Audubon F.R.S. F.L.S.

Engraved, Printed & Coloured by R. Havell.

PLATE CLXXIX.

Wood Wren,
TROGLODYTES AMERICANA
Male
Smilacina borealis

Drawn from Nature by J. J. Audubon F.R.S. F.L.S.

Engraved, Printed & Coloured by R. Havell, 1833.

PLATE CLXXX.

Pine Finch
FRINGILLA PINUS,
Male, I. Female, 2.
Pinus pendula. Black Larch.

Drawn from Nature by J. J. Audubon F.R.S. F.L.S

Engraved, Printed & Coloured by R. Havell, 1833.

PLATE CLXXXI.

Drawn from Nature by J. J. Audubon F.R.S. F.L.S.   *Golden Eagle* AQUILA CHRYSAETOS *Female adult. Northern Hare*   Engraved, Printed & Coloured by R. Havell, 1835

PLATE CLXXXII.

Ground Dove COLUMBA PASSERINA, Linn *Males 1 2 3. Female, 4. Young, 5. Wild Orange*

Drawn from Nature by J. J. Audubon F.R.S. F.L.S.

Engraved, Printed & Coloured by R. Havell, 1833.

PLATE CLXXXIII.

Golden crested-Wren REGULUS CRISTATUS. Viell. *Male,* I. *Female,* 2. *Thalia dealbata.*

Drawn from Nature by J. J. Audubon F.R.S. F.L.S.

Engraved, Printed & Coloured by R. Havell

Mangrove Humming Bird.

TROCHILUS MANGO.

Males, 1. 2. 3. Females, 4. 5.

Tecoma grandiflora.

Drawn from Nature by J. J. Audubon F.R.S. F.L.S.

Engraved, Printed & Coloured by R. Havell. 1833.

PLATE CLXXXV.

Bachman's Warbler, SYLVIA BACHMANII. Aud. *Male,*1. *Female,*2. *Gordonia pubescens.*

Drawn from Nature by J. J. Audubon F.R.S. F.L.S.

Engraved, Printed & Coloured by R. Havell, 1833.

PLATE CLXXXVI.

Engraved, Printed & Coloured by R. Havell. 1834

Pinnated Grous TETRAO CUPIDO. Lin   Males, 1,2. Female 3.   Lilium Superbum.

Drawn from Nature by J. J. Audubon F.R.S. L.S.

PLATE CLXXXVII.

Boat-tailed Grackle

QUISCALUS MAJOR, Vieill.
Male. 1. Female. 2.
Live Oak—Quercus virens.

Drawn from Nature by J. J. Audubon F.R.S. L.S.

Engraved, Printed & Coloured by R. Havell, 1834.

PLATE CLXXXVIII.

Tree Sparrow,
FRINGILLA CANADENSIS.Lath
Male,1. Female,2.
Berberis Canadensis.

Drawn from Nature by J. J. Audubon F.R.S. L.S.

Engraved, Printed & Coloured by R. Havell, 1834.

Snow Bunting.

EMBERIZA NIVALIS. Linn.
Adult, 1, 2. Young, 3.

Drawn from Nature by J. J. Audubon F.R.S. F.L.S.

Engraved, Printed & Coloured by R. Havell, 1834.

PLATE CXC.

Yellow bellied Woodpecker,

PICUS VARIUS. Linn.

Male, 1. Female, 2.

Prunus caroliniana.

Drawn from Nature by J. J. Audubon F.R.S. F.L.S.

Engraved, Printed & Coloured by R. Havell, 1834.

PLATE CXCI.

No. 39.

Willow Grous or Large Ptarmigan

TETRAO SALICETI. Temm.

Male. 1. Female. 2. & Young.

Labrador Tea. 1. Sweet pea. 2.

Drawn from Nature by J J Audubon F.R.S. F.L.S.

Engraved, Printed & Coloured by R. Havell 1834.

PLATE CXCII.

Great American Shrike or Butcher Bird LANIUS SEPTENTUONALIS *Male.1. F.2. Summer Plumage Do.3. Young or Winter Do. F.4. Crataegus apifolia*

Drawn from Nature by J. J. Audubon F.R.S. L.S.

Engraved, Printed & Coloured by R. Havell. 1834.

Lincoln Finch,

FRINGILLA LINCOLNII.
Male, 1. Female, 2.

Drawn from Nature by J. J. Audubon F.R.S. F.L.S.

1, *Cornus Suifsica,* 2, *Rubus Chamarus,* 3, *Kalmia glauca.*

Engraved, Printed & Coloured by R. Havell, 1834.

Canadian Titmouse,

PARUS HUDSONICUS.
Male, 1. Female, 2. Young, 3.

Drawn from Nature by J. J. Audubon F.R.S. F.L.S.

Engraved, Printed & Coloured by R. Havell, 1834

PLATE CXCV.

Ruby crowned Wren,

REGULUS CALENDULA. Stephens
Male, 1. Female, 2. Summer plumage.
Kalmia Angustifolia.

Drawn from Nature by J. J. Audubon F.R.S. F.L.S.

Engraved, Printed & Coloured by R. Havell, 1834.

PLATE CXCVI.

Labrador Falcon

FALCO LABRADORA
Male, 1. Female, 2. adult

Drawn from Nature by J. J. Audubon F.R.S. F.L.S.

Engraved, Printed & Coloured by R. Havell, 1834.

American Crossbill LOXIA CURVIROSTRA, Linn.
Male adult, 1. Young Male, 2, 3. Female adult, 4. Young Female, 5. Hemlock

Drawn from Nature by J. J. Audubon F.R.S. L.S.

Engraved, Printed & Coloured by R. Havell, 1834.

Bill hind toe with claw of the Sylvia vermivora.

Bill hind toe & claw of the present species.

Brown headed Worm eating Warbler,
SYLVIA SWAINSONII.
Azalia Calendula – Orange coloured Azalia.

Drawn from Nature by J. J. Audubon F.R.S. F.L.S.

Engraved, Printed & Coloured by R. Havell.

Little Owl,

STRIX ACADICA. Gm.
Male, I. *Female,* 2.
Common Mouse.

Drawn from Nature by J. J. Audubon F.R.S. F.L.S.

Engraved, Printed & Coloured by R. Havell, 1834.

Shore Lark.

ALAUDA ALPESTRIS. Z.

Male adult Summer plumage, 1. F. 2. Male Winter plumage, 3 Young, 4, 5, 6.

Drawn from Nature by J. J. Audubon F.R.S. F.L.S.

Engraved, Printed & Coloured by R. Havell

PLATE CCI.

Canada Goose

ANSER CANADENSIS. Vieill

Male, I. Female, 2.

Drawn from Nature by J. J. Audubon F.R.S. F.L.S.

Engraved, Printed & Coloured by R. Havell.

PLATE CCII.

Drawn from Nature by J.J. Audubon FRS. FLS.

Red-throated Diver. COLYMBUS SEPTENTRIONALIS. *Male adult summer plumage1. Do. Winter plumage.2. Adult Female 3. Young 4*

Engraved, Printed & Coloured by R. Havell 1834.

PLATE CCIII.

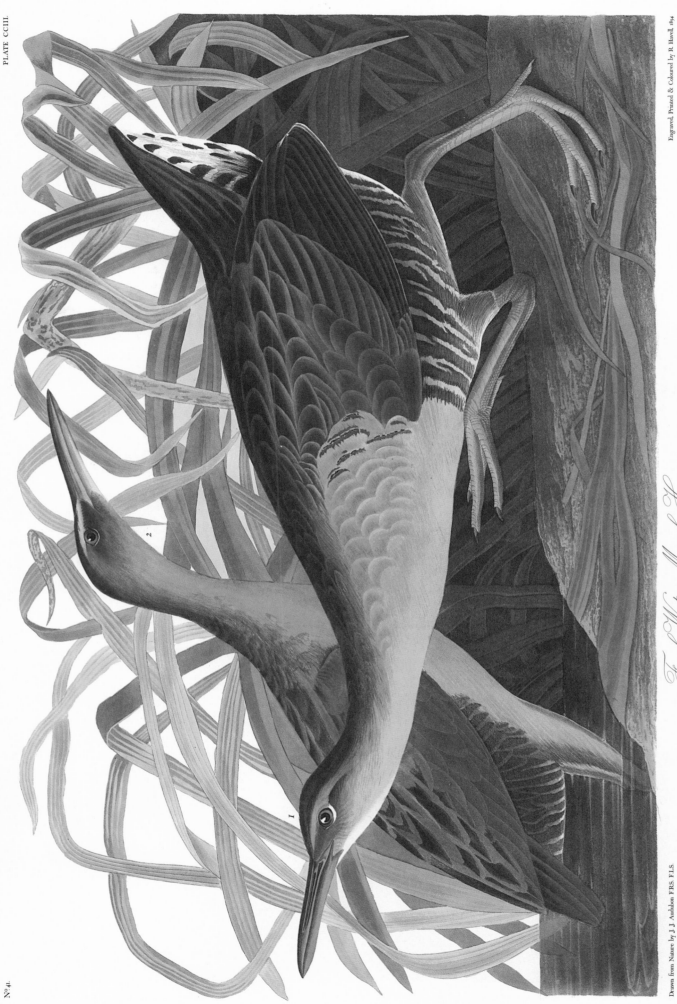

Engraved, Printed & Coloured by R. Havell 1854

Fresh Water Marsh Hen RALLUS ELEGANS. And *Male spring plumage.1. Young autumnal plumage.2.*

Drawn from Nature by J. J. Audubon F.R.S. F.L.S.

Drawn from Nature by J. J. Audubon F.R.S. F.L.S.

Engraved, Printed & Coloured by R. Havell 1834

Salt Water Marsh Hen RALLUS CREPITANS, Gm. *1, Male adult spring plumage. 2, Female.*

PLATE CCV.

N°4.

Virginia Rail. RALLUS VIRGINIANUS.L. *Male.1. Female.2. Young autumnal plumage.3*

Drawn from Nature by J. J. Audubon F.R.S. F.L.S.

Engraved, Printed & Coloured by R. Havell 1834

Summer or Wood Duck

ANAS SPONSA. L.

1, 2, Males. 3, 4, Females.

Platanus occidentalis. - Button Wood Tree

Drawn from Nature by J. J. Audubon F.R.S. F.L.S.

Engraved, Printed & Coloured by R. Havell, 1834.

Drawn from Nature by J. J. Audubon F.R.S. F.L.S.

Booby Gannet
SULA FUSCA

Engraved, Printed & Coloured by R. Havell, 1834

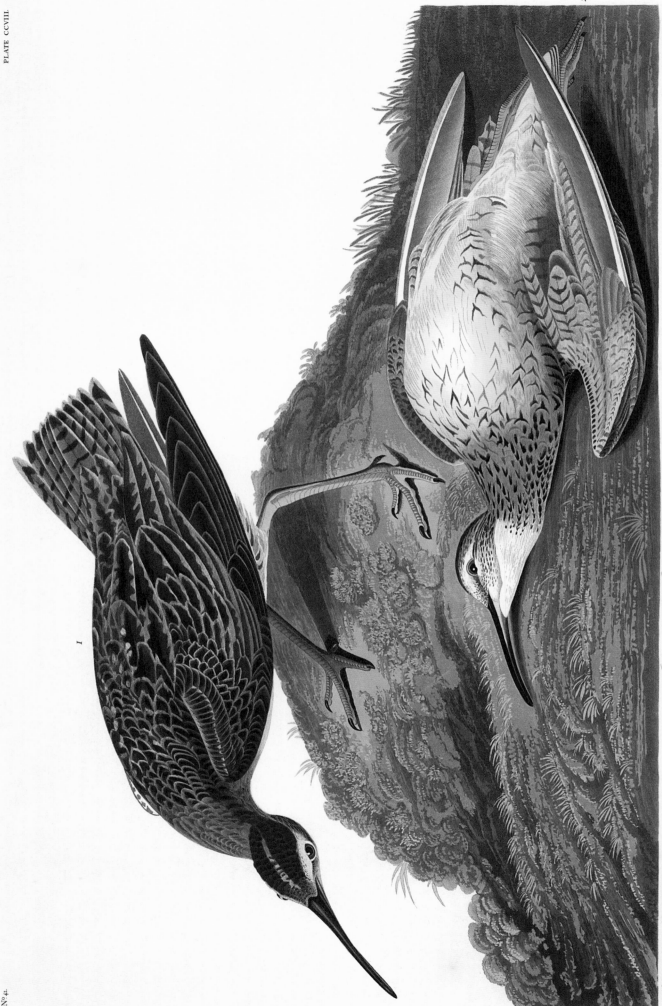

Esquimaux Curlew, NUMENIUS BOREALIS. Lath, Male, 1. Female, 2.

PLATE CCIX.

Drawn from Nature by J. J. Audubon F.R.S. F.L.S.

Engraved, Printed & Coloured by R. Havell 1834

Wilson's Plover CHARADRIUS WILSONIUS *1. Male. 2. Female.*

PLATE CCX.

Drawn from Nature by J. J. Audubon F.R.S. F.L.S.

Least Bittern. ARDEA EXILIS. Gm. 1. Male. 2. Female. 3. Young.

Engraved, Printed & Coloured by R. Havell 1834

Drawn from Nature by J. J. Audubon F.R.S. F.L.S.

Engraved, Printed & Coloured by R. Havell, 1834.

Great blue Heron ARDEA HERODIAS *Male*

PLATE CCXII.

Drawn from Nature by J. J. Audubon F.R.S. F.L.S.

Engraved, Printed & Coloured by R. Havell. 1834.

Common Gull LARUS CANUS I. Adult. 2. Young.

PLATE CCXIII.

Drawn from Nature by J. J. Audubon FRS. FLS.

Engraved, Printed & Coloured by R Havell 1834

Puffin. MORMON ARCTICUS. *1. Male. 2. Female.*

PLATE CCXIV.

Drawn from Nature by J.J. Audubon FRS FLS.

Razor Bill. ALCA TORDA. 1.Male. 2.Female.

Engraved, Printed & Coloured by R. Havell 1834

PLATE CCXV.

Drawn from Nature by J J Audubon FRS FLS

Hyperborean phalarope. PHALAROPUS HYPERBOREUS. Lath. 1. Male adult spring plumage. 2. Female Do. 3. Young autumnal plumage.

Engraved, Printed & Coloured by R. Havell 1834

PLATE CCXVI.

Drawn from Nature by J. J. Audubon F.R.S. F.L.S.

Engraved, Printed & Coloured by R. Havell, 1834

Wood Ibiss TANTALUS LOCULATOR

PLATE CCXVII.

Drawn from Nature by J.J. Audubon F.R.S. F.L.S.

Engraved, Printed & Coloured by R. Havell 1834

Louisiana Heron ARDEA LUDOVICIANA, Wils. *Male adult*

PLATE CXVIII.

Engraved, Printed & Coloured by R. Havell 1834

Foolish Guillemot, *URIA TROILE. Lath.* 1. Adult summer plumage Male. 2. Female.

Drawn from Nature by J. J. Audubon FRS. FLS.

PLATE CCXIX.

Drawn from Nature by J. J. Audubon FRS. FLS.

Engraved, Printed & Coloured by R. Havell 1834

Black Guillemot

URIA GRYLLE, Lath.

1. Adult summer plumage. 2. Do. Winter plumage. 3. Young.

PLATE CCXX

Drawn from Nature by J. J. Audubon F.R.S. F.L.S.

Engraved, Printed & Coloured by R. Havell 1834.

Piping Plover, CHARADRIUS MELODUS 1. Male. 2. Female.

No. 45. PLATE CCXXI.

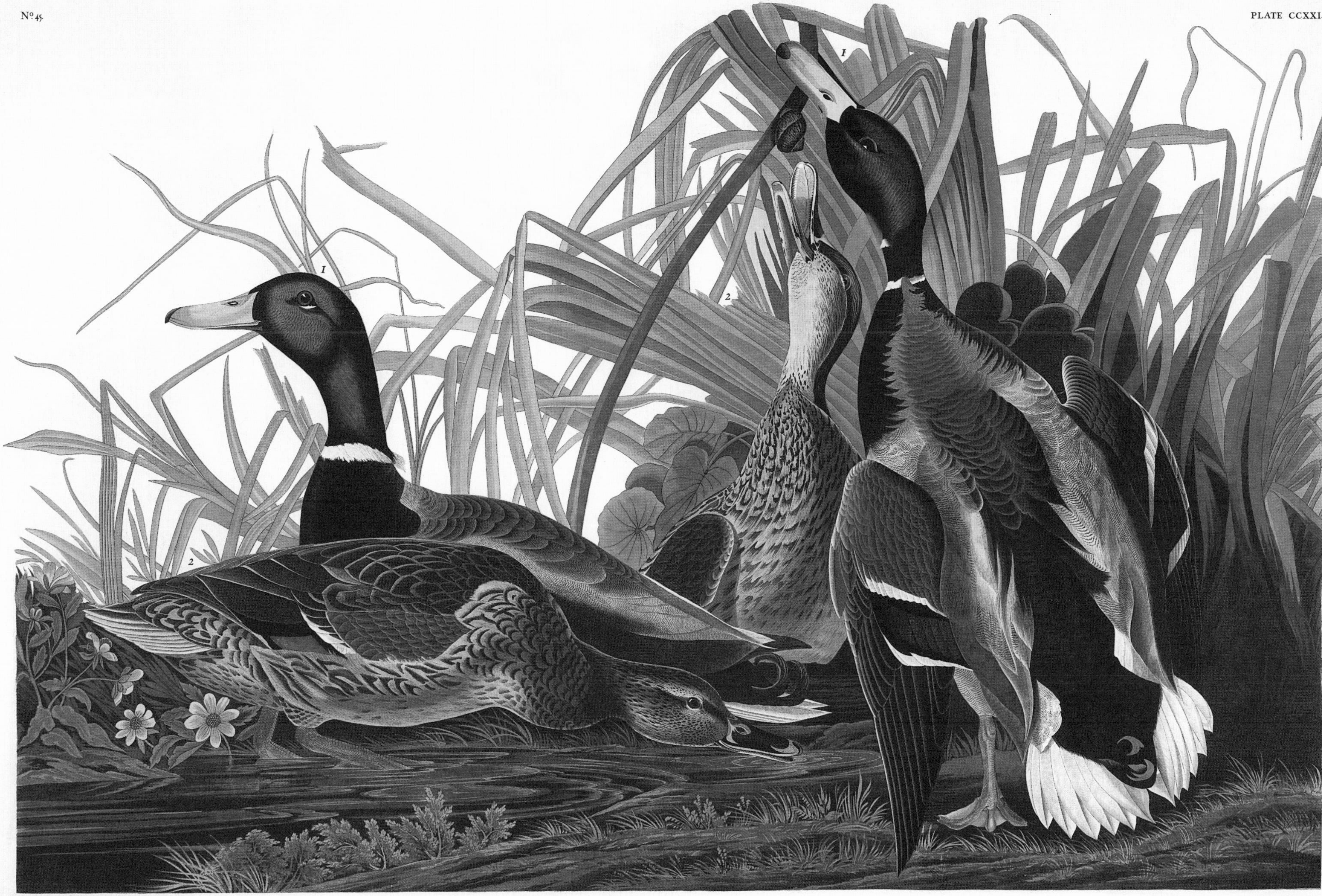

Drawn from Nature by J. J. Audubon F.R.S. F.L.S.

Engraved, Printed & Coloured by R. Havell, 1834

Mallard Duck ANAS BOSCHAS. L. *1. Males. 2. Females*

PLATE CCXXII.

Drawn from Nature by J. J. Audubon F.R.S. F.L.S.

White Ibis IBIS ALBA 1. Adult 2. Young in Autumn

Engraved, Printed & Coloured by R. Havell 1834

PLATE CCXXIII.

No 45.

Engraved, Printed & Coloured by R. Havell. 1834

Pied oyster-catcher, HÆMATOPUS OSTRALEGUS. L.

Drawn from Nature by J. J. Audubon FRS. FLS.

PLATE CCXXIV.

1

2

Drawn from Nature by J. J. Audubon F.R.S. F.L.S.

Engraved, Printed & Coloured by R. Havell 1834

Kittiwake Gull. LARUS TRIDACTYLUS. L. *1. Adult. 2. Young.*

PLATE CCXXV.

Engraved, Printed & Coloured by R. Havell 1834

Kildeer Plover. CHARADRIUS VOCIFERUS *1. Male. 2. Female.*

Drawn from Nature by J J Audubon FRS. F.L.S.

Hooping Crane GRUS AMERICANA *Adult Male*

PLATE CCXVII.

Drawn from Nature by J. J. Audubon F.R.S. F.L.S.

Pin tailed Duck ANAS ACUTA Male 1. Female 2.

Engraved, Printed & Coloured by R Havell, 1834.

PLATE CCXXVIII.

1

2

Drawn from Nature by J. J. Audubon F.R.S. F.L.S.

Engraved, Printed & Coloured by R. Havell 1834

American Green winged Teal ANAS CAROLINENSIS. Lath   1. Male. 2. Female.

PLATE CCXXIX

Engraved, Printed & Coloured by R. Havell 1834

Drawn from Nature by J. J. Audubon F.R.S. F.L.S.

Scaup Duck. FULIGULA MARILA. *1 Male 2 Female*

PLATE CCXXX.

Drawn from Nature by J. J. Audubon FRS. FLS.

Ruddy Plover. TRINGA ARENARIA. *1. Male. 2. Female.*

Engraved, Printed & Coloured by R. Havell 1834.

PLATE CCXXXI.

Drawn from Nature by J. J. Audubon FRS. FLS.

Long-billed Curlew NUMENIUS LONGIROSTRIS. *1. Male. 2. Female. City of Charleston.*

Engraved, Printed & Coloured by R. Havell, 1834.

PLATE CCXXXII.

Drawn from Nature by J J Audubon F.R.S. F.L.S.

Hooded Merganser MERGUS CUCULLATUS 1. Male. 2. Female.

Engraved, Printed & Coloured by R. Havell 1834

PLATE CCXXXIII.

Drawn from Nature by J. J. Audubon F.R.S. F.L.S.

Sora or Rail. RALLUS CAROLINUS. L. 1. Male. 2. Female. 3. Young.

Engraved, Printed & Coloured by R. Havell 1834

PLATE CCXXXIV.

Drawn from Nature by J. J. Audubon FRS. FLS.

Tufted Duck. FULIGULA RUFITORQUES. Bonap *1. Male. 2. Female.*

Engraved, Printed & Coloured by R. Havell 1834

Engraved, Printed & Coloured by R. Havell 1834

Sooty Tern, STERNA FULIGINOSA

Drawn from Nature by J. J. Audubon F.R.S. F.L.S.

PLATE CCXXXVI.

Engraved, Printed & Coloured by R. Havell, 1835

Night Heron or Qua bird ARDEA NYCTICORAX, L. Adult 1. and Young 2.

Drawn from Nature by J. J. Audubon F.R.S. F.L.S.

PLATE CCXXXVII.

Drawn from Nature by J. J. Audubon F.R.S. F.L.S.

Great Esquimaux Curlew
NUMENIUS HUDSONICUS, LATH

Engraved, Printed & Coloured by R. Havell 1835

PLATE CCXXXVIII.

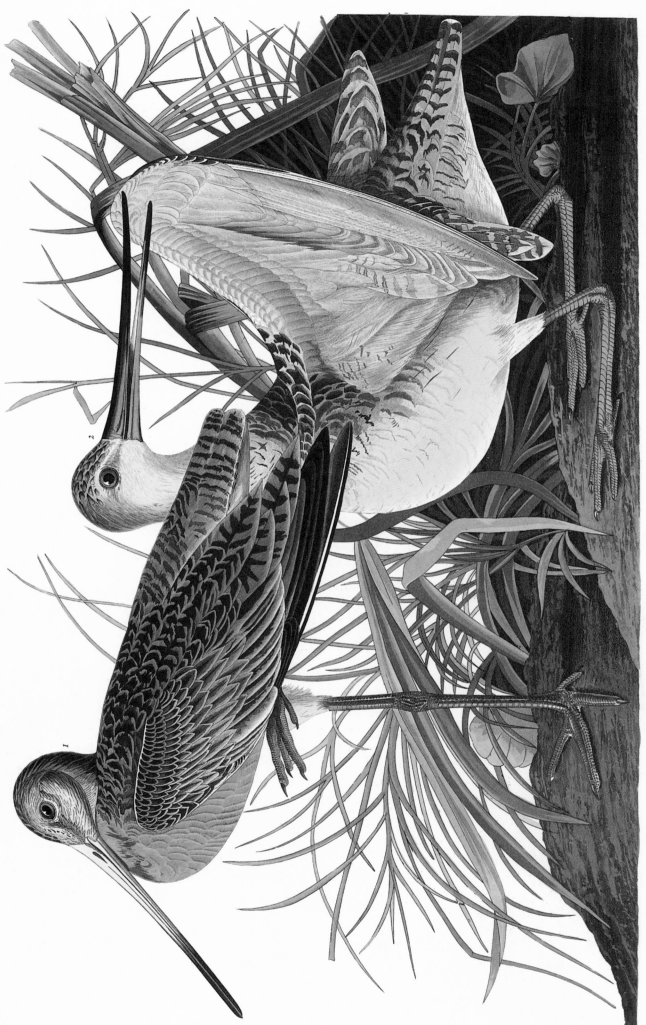

Engraved, Printed & Coloured by R. Havell. London 1835.

Great Marbled Godwit. 1 Male. 2 Female.

LIMOSA FEDOA, Vieill.

Drawn from Nature by J. J. Audubon. F.R.S. F.L.S.

PLATE CCXXXIX.

Drawn from Nature by J. J. Audubon F.R.S. F.L.S.

Engraved, Printed & Coloured by R Havell, London 1835

American Coot.

FULICA AMERICANA. GM.

Drawn from Nature by J. J. Audubon F.R.S. F.L.S.

Engraved, Printed & Coloured by R. Havell, London 1835.

Roseate Tern.

STERNA DOUGALLII. MONT.

Black Backed Gull

LARUS MARINUS

Snowy Heron or White Egret ARDEA CANDIDISSIMA, Gm.
Male adult Spring plumage.
Rice plantation. South Carolina.

Drawn from Nature by J. J. Audubon F.R.S. F.L.S.

Engraved, Printed & Coloured by R. Havell. 1835.

PLATE CCXLIII.

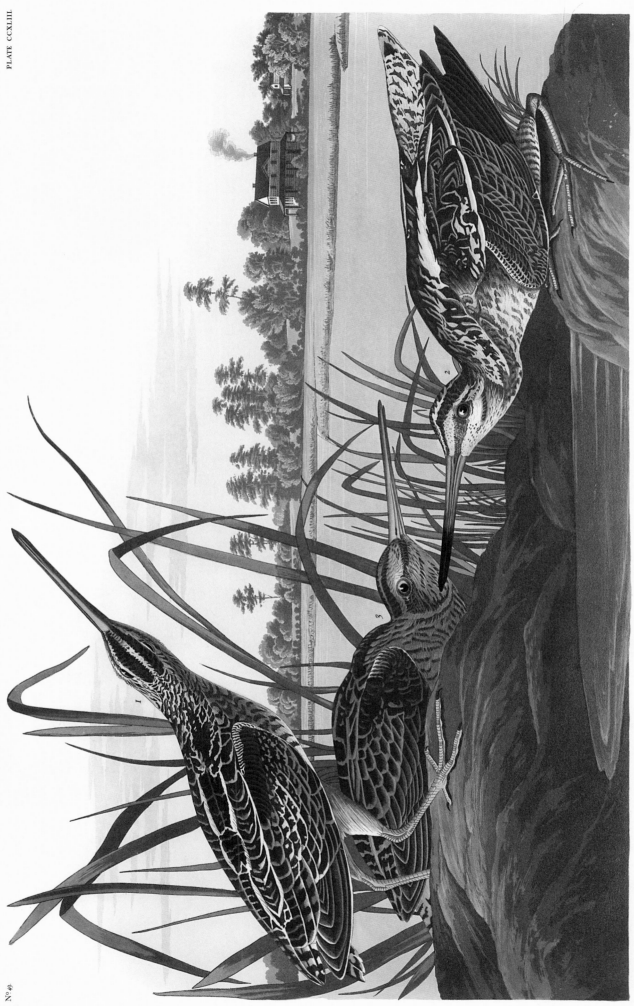

Drawn from Nature by J. J. Audubon F.R.S. F.L.S.

Engraved, Printed & Coloured by R. Havell, London 1835.

American Snipe. Male 1. Female 2.3.

SCOLOPAX WILSONII, *South Carolina Plantation, near Charleston.*

PLATE CCXLIV.

Drawn from Nature by J. J. Audubon F.R.S. F.L.S.

Engraved, Printed & Coloured by R. Havell, London 1835.

Common Gallinule, Male. Adult. GALLINULA CHLOROPUS.

PLATE CCXLV.

Drawn from Nature by J J Audubon F.R.S. F.L.S.

URIA BRUNNICHII

Engraved, Printed & Coloured by R Havell, London. 1835

PLATE CCXLVI.

Engraved, Printed & Coloured by R Havell London 1835

Eider Duck

FULIGULA MOLLISSIMA, Male 1. Female 2.

Drawn from Nature by J J Audubon FRS. FLS.

PLATE CCXLVII.

Drawn from Nature by J. J. Audubon FRS. FLS.

Engraved, Printed & Coloured by R. Havell. London 1835.

Velvet Duck

FULIGULA FUSCA *Male 1. Female 2.*

PLATE CCXLVIII

Drawn from Nature by J. J. Audubon F.R.S. F.L.S.

Engraved, Printed & Coloured by R. Havell London 1835

American Pied-bill Dobchick

PODICEPS CAROLINENSIS.

PLATE CCXLIX.

Tufted Auk.

MORMON CIRRHATUS, Lath. *Male.1. Female.2.*

Drawn from Nature by J. J. Audubon F.R.S. F.L.S.

Engraved, Printed & Coloured by R. Havell London 1835

Drawn from Nature by J. J. Audubon F.R.S. F.L.S.

Engraved, Printed & Coloured by R. Havell, London 1835

Arctic Tern

STERNA ARCTICA

Brown Pelican

PELECANUS FUSCUS
Male Adult

Drawn from Nature by J. J. Audubon F.R.S. F.L.S.

Engraved, Printed & Coloured by R. Havell, 1835.

PLATE CCLII.

Drawn from Nature by J. J. Audubon F.R.S. F.L.S.

Engraved, Printed & Coloured by R. Havell 1835

Florida Cormorant
CARBO FLORIDANUS
Male Adult. Spring Dress. View Florida Keys.

PLATE CCLIII.

Drawn from Nature by J. J. Audubon F.R.S. F.L.S.

Jager

LESTRIS POMARINA, Temm.

Engraved, Printed & Coloured by R. Havell 1835

PLATE CCLVI.

Wilson's Phalarope.

PHALAROPUS WILSONII, Sabine. *Male Adult.1, Female 2.*

PLATE CCLV.

Drawn from Nature by J. J. Audubon FRS. F.L.S.

Red Phalarope

PHALAROPUS PLATYRHYNCHUS, Temm. Adult Male 1. Adult Female 2. Winter Plumage 3.

Engraved, Printed & Coloured by R. Havell 1835

PLATE CCLVI.

Drawn from Nature by J. J. Audubon FRS. FLS.

Engraved, Printed & Coloured by R. Havell 1835

Purple Heron
ARDEA RUFESCENS, Buff
Adult full spring plumage. 1. Young two Years old in spring plumage. 2.

PLATE CCLVII.

Drawn from Nature by J. J. Audubon F.R.S. F.L.S.

Engraved, Printed & Coloured by R. Havell, 1835

Double-crested Cormorant

PHALACROCORAX DILOPHUS, Swain & Richards

Male adult spring plumage

PLATE CCLVIII.

Drawn from Nature by J. J. Audubon FRS. FLS.

Hudsonian Godwit.

LIMOSA HUDSONICA. Swain & Richard's Male 1. Young Female 2. Summer plumage.

Engraved, Printed & Coloured by R. Havell 1835

PLATE CCLIX.

N°52.

Drawn from Nature by J. J. Audubon FRS FLS

Engraved, Printed & Coloured by R. Havell 1835

Horned Grebe

PODICEPS CORNUTUS, Lath.

Adult Male,1. Female Winter plumage,2.

PLATE CCXL.

1

2

Drawn from Nature by J. J. Audubon FRS FLS

Engraved, Printed & Coloured by R. Havell. London 1835.

Fork-tail Petrel

THALASSIDROMA LEACHII, *Male 1, Female 2.*

PLATE CCLXI.

Drawn from Nature by J. J. Audubon F.R.S. F.L.S.

Engraved, Printed & Coloured by R. Havell, 1835.

Hooping Crane
GRUS AMERICANA
Young.
View in the Interior of the Floridas with sand Hills in the distance

PLATE CCLXII.

Drawn from Nature by J. J. Audubon F.R.S. F.L.S.

Engraved, Printed & Coloured by R. Havell. 1835.

Tropic Bird
PHAETON ÆTHEREUS, Linn.
Male 1. Female 2.

PLATE CCLXIII.

Drawn from Nature by J. J. Audubon FRS FLS.

Engraved, Printed & Coloured by R. Havell 1835

Pigmy Curlew

TRINGA SUBARQUATA. Temm

Adult Male.1. Young.2.

PLATE CCLXIV.

Fulmar Petrel
PROCELLARIA GLACIALIS, L.
Male adult Summer plumage.

Drawn from Nature by J. J. Audubon FRS. FLS.

Engraved, Printed & Coloured by R. Havell 1835

PLATE CCLXV.

Drawn from Nature by J. J. Audubon FRS FLS.

Buff breasted Sandpiper.
TRINGA RUFESCENS. Viell
1. Male. 2. Female.

Engraved, Printed & Coloured by R. Havell 1835

PLATE CCLXVI.

Drawn from Nature by J. J. Audubon F.R.S. F.L.S.

Engraved, Printed & Coloured by R. Havell 1835

Common Cormorant

PHALACROCORAX CARBO, Dumont

Male adult spring plumage. 1. Female. 2. Young. 3.

PLATE CCLXVII.

Arctic Yager

Drawn from Nature by J. J. Audubon F.R.S. F.L.S.

Engraved, Printed & Coloured by R. Havell, 1835

Arctic Yager

LESTRIS PARASITICA

PLATE CCLXVIII.

Drawn from Nature by J. J. Audubon F.R.S. F.L.S.

American Woodcock

SCOLOPAX MINOR, Gmel. Male 1. Female 2. Young Autumn. 3.

Engraved, Printed & Coloured by R. Havell. London 1835.

PLATE CCLXIX.

Drawn from Nature by J. J. Audubon F.R.S. F.L.S.

Greenshank

TOTANUS GLOTTIS. Temm. *View of St. Augustine & Spanish Fort East Florida*

Engraved, Printed & Coloured by R. Havell. 1835

PLATE CCLXX.

Drawn from Nature by J. J. Audubon F.R.S. F.L.S.

Stormy Petrel

THALASSIDROMA WILSONII, *Male 1. Female 2.*

Engraved, Printed & Coloured by R. Havell London 1835

Frigate Pelican
TACHYPETES AQUILUS. Viel.
Male Adult

Drawn from Nature by J. J. Audubon F.R.S. F.L.S.

Engraved, Printed & Coloured by R. Havell, 1835.

PLATE CCLXXII.

Drawn from Nature by J. J. Audubon F.R.S. F.L.S.

Richardson's Jager LESTRIS RICHARDSONII Male adult 1. Young in Sepr. 2.

Engraved, Printed & Coloured by R. Havell 1835.

PLATE CCLXXIII.

Engraved, Printed & Coloured by R. Havell. London 1835.

Cayenne Tern.
STERNA CAYANA, Lath.
Male Adult. Spring plumage.

Drawn from Nature by J. J. Audubon FRS F.LS.

PLATE CCLXIV.

Drawn from Nature by J. J. Audubon FRS. FLS

Engraved, Printed & Coloured by R. Havell, London 1835.

Semipalmated Snipe, or Willet.

TOTANUS SEMIPALMATUS, Temm. Male Adult Spring plumage 1, Female Adult Winter plumage 2.

PLATE CCLXXV.

Drawn from Nature by J. J. Audubon FRS FLS.

Engraved, Printed & Coloured by R. Havell, London 1835.

Noddy Tern
STERNA STOLIDA, L.
Male Adult

PLATE CCLXXVI.

King Duck
FULIGULA SPECTABILIS, Lath.
Male.1. Female, 2.

Drawn from Nature by J. J. Audubon F.R.S. F.L.S.

Engraved, Printed & Coloured by R. Havell 1835

Drawn from Nature by J. J. Audubon F.R.S. F.L.S.

Hutchins's Barnacle Goose

ANSER HUTCHINSII, Richd. & Swain.

Engraved, Printed & Coloured by R. Havell, 1835.

PLATE CCLXXVII.

Drawn from Nature by J. J. Audubon F.R.S. F.L.S.

Schinz's Sandpiper.
TRINGA SCHINZII. Brehm.
View on the East Coast of Florida.

Engraved, Printed & Coloured by R. Havell 1835

PLATE CCLXXIX.

Drawn from Nature by J. J. Audubon F.R.S. F.L.S.

Sandwich Tern

STERNA BOYSSII. Lath.

Florida. Cray Fish

Engraved, Printed & Coloured by R. Havell 1835

Drawn from Nature by J. J. Audubon F.R.S. F.L.S.

Engraved, Printed & Coloured by R. Havell, 1835.

Black Tern

STERNA NIGRA. Lin.
Adult, 1. Young in Autumn, 2.

PLATE CCLXXXI.

Drawn from Nature by J. J. Audubon FRS. FLS.

Engraved, Printed & Coloured by R. Havell, 1835.

Great White Heron ARDEA OCCIDENTALIS *Male adult spring plumage* View Key-west.

PLATE CCLXXXII.

Drawn from Nature by J. J. Audubon F.R.S. F.L.S.

Engraved, Printed & Coloured by R. Havell 1855

White-winged silvery Gull. LARUS LEUCOPTERUS, Bonap. 1 Male summer plumage. 2 Young in Winter.

PLATE CCLXXXIII.

Drawn from Nature by J. J. Audubon FRS. FLS.

Engraved, Printed & Coloured by R. Havell 1835

Wandering Shearwater

PUFFINUS CINEREUS. Bonap. *Male.*

PLATE CCLXXXIV.

Purple Sandpiper.
TRINGA MARITIMA, Bonap.
1. Male Summer plumage. 2. Female Winter. 3. Charadrius Wilsonius.

Drawn from Nature by J.J. Audubon F.R.S. F.L.S.

Engraved, Printed & Coloured by R. Havell 1833.

PLATE CCLXXXV.

Fork-tailed Gull.

LARUS SABINI, Swain & Richards.

1. Male Summer plumage. 2.Tringa. arenaria. Male Spring plumage.

Drawn from Nature by J. J. Audubon F.R.S. F.L.S.

Engraved, Printed & Coloured by R. Havell 1835.

PLATE CCLXXXVI.

Drawn from Nature by J.J. Audubon F.R.S. F.L.S.

Engraved, Printed & Coloured by R. Havell. 1836

White-fronted Goose, Lath.
ANSER ALBIFRONS, Bechst
1.Male. 2.Female.

PLATE CCLXXXVII.

Drawn from Nature by J.J. Audubon F.R.S. F.L.S.

Engraved, Printed & Coloured by R. Havell 1835

Ivory Gull, Leek

LARUS EBURNEUS, Gm. 1 Adult Male. 2 Young Second Autumn.

PLATE CCLXXVIII

Yellow Shank.
TOTANUS FLAVIPES, Vieill.
Male Summer plumage.
View in South Carolina.

Drawn from Nature by J. J. Audubon F.R.S. F.L.S.

Engraved, Printed & Coloured by R. Havell 1836.

PLATE CCLXXXIX.

Drawn from Nature by J. J. Audubon F.R.S. F.L.S.

Engraved, Printed & Coloured by R. Havell 1835

Solitary Sandpiper.
TOTANUS CHLOROPYGIUS, Viell *1.Male. 2.Female.*

PLATE CCXC.

No. 9

Drawn from Nature by J. J. Audubon FRS. FLS.

Engraved, Printed & Coloured by R. Havell 1855.

Red backed Sandpiper.

TRINGA ALPINA. L. 1. Summer plumage. 2. Winter plumage.

Drawn from Nature by J. J. Audubon F.R.S. F.L.S.

Engraved, Printed & Coloured by R. Havell, 1836.

Herring Gull
LARUS ARGENTATUS. Brunn.
1. Adult Male Spring plumage. 2. Young in November.
Raccoon Oysters & View of the entrance into St. Augustine

PLATE CCXCII.

N.º 59.

1

2

Drawn from Nature by J. J. Audubon F.R.S. F.L.S.

Engraved, Printed & Coloured by R. Havell 1836.

Crested Grebe
PODICEPS CRISTATUS, Lath.
Adult Male spring plumage. 1. Young first Winter. 2.

PLATE CCXCIII.

Drawn from Nature by J. J. Audubon F.R.S. F.L.S.

Large billed Puffin
MORMON GLACIALIS, Leach
1. Male. 2. Female.

Engraved, Printed & Coloured by R. Havell, 1836.

PLATE CCXCIV.

Drawn from Nature by J. J. Audubon FRS. FLS.

Engraved, Printed & Coloured by R. Havell 1836

Pectoral Sandpiper
TRINGA PECTORALIS
1.Male. 2.Female.

PLATE CCXCV.

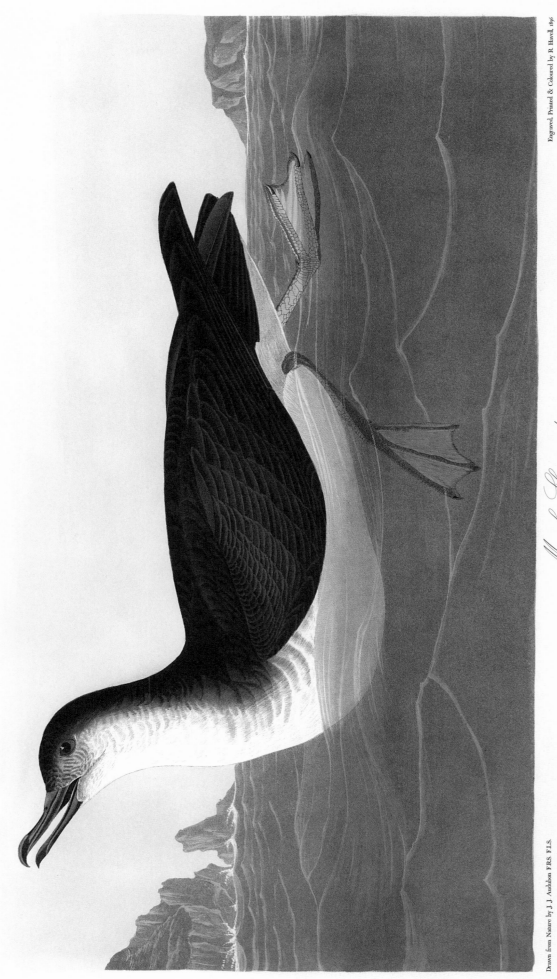

Drawn from Nature by J. J. Audubon F.R.S. F.L.S.

Engraved, Printed & Coloured by R. Havell 1836.

Manks Shearwater

PUFFINUS ANGLORUM, Ray

Male Bird

PLATE CCXCVI.

Drawn from Nature by J. J. Audubon F.R.S. F.L.S.

Engraved, Printed & Coloured by R. Havell 1846

Barnacle Goose
ANSER LEUCOPSIS,
1. Male. 2. Female.

PLATE CCXCVII.

Drawn from Nature by J. J. Audubon F.R.S. F.L.S.

Engraved, Printed & Coloured by R. Havell 1845

Harlequin Duck
FULIGULA HISTRIONICA, Bonap.
1 Old Male. 2 Female. 3 Young Male third year.

PLATE CCXCVIII.

Drawn from Nature by J. J. Audubon FRS. FLS.

Engraved, Printed & Coloured by R. Havell 1836

Red-necked Grebe

PODICEPS RUBRICOLLIS, Lath. *1. Adult Male spring plumage. 2. Winter plumage.*

PLATE CCXCIX.

Engraved, Printed & Coloured by R Havell. 1836

Dusky Petrel. Leach
PUFFINUS OBSCURUS, Cuvier
Made in Spring

Drawn from Nature by J. J. Audubon FRS. FLS.

PLATE CCC.

Drawn from Nature by J. J. Audubon FRS. F.L.S.

Engraved, Printed & Coloured by R. Havell. 1846

Golden Plover

CHARADRIUS PLUVIALIS.L. 1 Summer plumage. 2 Winter. 3 Variety in. March.

PLATE CCCI.

Drawn from Nature by J. J. Audubon F.R.S. F.L.S.

Engraved, Printed & Coloured by R. Havell 1836.

Canvas backed Duck
FULIGULA VALLISNERIA. Steph
1 2. Male 3 Female.
View of Baltimore

PLATE CCCII.

Drawn from Nature by J. J. Audubon FRS. FLS.

Dusky Duck

ANAS OBSCURA. Gm 1.Male. 2.Female.

Engraved, Printed & Coloured by R. Havell 1836.

PLATE CCCIII.

Engraved, Printed & Coloured by R. Havell 1836

Bartram Sandpiper
TOTANUS BARTRAMIUS. Temm
1. Male. 2. Female.

Drawn from Nature by J. J. Audubon FRS. FLS.

PLATE CCCIV.

Drawn from Nature by J. J. Audubon FRS FLS.

Turn-stone.

STREPSILAS INTERPRES. III 1. Summer plumage. 2. Winter.

Engraved, Printed & Coloured by R. Havell. 1835.

PLATE CCCV.

Nº 61.

Engraved, Printed & Coloured by R. Havell, 1836

Purple Gallinule.
GALLINULA MARTINICA. Gmel
Adult Male spring plumage.

Drawn from Nature by J. J. Audubon FRS FLS.

PLATE CCCVI.

Drawn from Nature by J. J. Audubon FRS. FLS.

Engraved, Printed & Coloured by R. Havell, 1836.

Great Northern Diver or Loon

COLYMBUS GLACIALIS, L.

Adult 1 Young in Winter 2.

PLATE CCCVII.

Blue Crane, or Heron

ARDEA CŒRULEA 1. Adult Male spring plumage. 2. Young second Year.
View near Charlestone S.C.

Drawn from Nature by J.J. Audubon F.R.S. F.L.S.

Engraved, Printed & Coloured by R. Havell 1836

PLATE CCCVII.

Drawn from Nature by J. J. Audubon F.R.S. F.L.S.

Tell-tale Godwit or Snipe.

TOTANUS MELANOLEUCUS, VIEILL. Male 1. F 2. *View in East Florida.*

Engraved, Printed & Coloured by R. Havell 1836.

Drawn from Nature by J. J. Audubon F.R.S. F.L.S.

Engraved, Printed & Coloured by R. Havell, 1836

Great Tern,
STERNA HIRUNDO, L.
Male Spring Plumage.

PLATE CCCX

Drawn from Nature by J. J. Audubon F.R.S. F.L.S.

Engraved, Printed & Coloured by R. Havell 1836

Spotted Sandpiper

TOTANUS MACULARIUS. 1. Adult Male. 2. Female. View on Bayou Sarah Louisiana.

PLATE CCCXI.

Drawn from Nature by J. J. Audubon F.R.S. F.L.S.

Engraved, Printed & Coloured by R. Havell, 1836.

American White Pelican

PELICANUS AMERICANUS, Aud.

Male Adult

PLATE CCCXII.

Drawn from Nature by J. J. Audubon F.R.S. F.L.S.

Engraved, Printed & Coloured by R. Havell 1836.

Long-tailed Duck

FULIGULA GLACIALIS 1 Male, summer plumage. 2 Male winter. 3 Female young.

PLATE CCCXIII.

Drawn from Nature by J.J Audubon FRS FLS.

Engraved, Printed & Coloured by R. Havell 1836.

Blue-Winged Teal.

ANAS DISCORS, L.

Male 1. Female 2.

PLATE CCCXIV.

Drawn from Nature by J. J. Audubon FRS. FLS.

Engraved, Printed & Coloured by R. Havell 1846

Black-headed Gull.
LARUS ATRICILLA. L.
Adult Male Spring Plumage 1. Young bird. Autumn 2.

PLATE CCCXV.

Drawn from Nature by J. J. Audubon F.R.S. F.L.S.

Red-breasted Sandpiper.
TRINGA ISLANDICA, L.
Summer Plumage 1. Winter 2.

Engraved, Printed & Coloured by R. Havell 1836.

PLATE CCCXVI.

Drawn from Nature by J. J. Audubon F.R.S. F.L.S.

Engraved, Printed & Coloured by R. Havell, 1836.

Black-bellied Darter

PLOTUS ANHINGA, L.

PLATE CCCXVI.

Drawn from Nature by J. J. Audubon FRS. FLS.

Black, or Surf Duck.
FULIGULA PERSPICILLATA Male Adult 1. Female 2.

Engraved, Printed and Coloured by R. Havell 1836

PLATE CCCXVII.

Drawn from Nature by J.J. Audubon F.R.S. F.L.S.

American Avocet.
RECURVIROSTRA AMERICANA.
Young in first Winter Plumage I
Adult 2

Engraved, Printed & Coloured by R. Havell. 1836

Lesser Tern,
STERNA MINUTA, L.
Adult Spring Plumage 1. Young in Sepr. 2.

PLATE CCCXX.

Drawn from Nature by J J Audubon FRS FLS.

Engraved, Printed & Coloured by R. Havell. 1836.

Little Sandpiper.

TRINGA PUSILLA, WILS. Male Adult Summer plumage I. F. 2.

PLATE CCCXXI.

Engraved, Printed and Coloured by R. Havell 1836

Roseate Spoonbill
PLATALEA AJAJA, L.
Male Adult

Drawn from Nature by J J Audubon FRS FLS

PLATE CCCXXII

Drawn from Nature by J.J. Audubon FRS. FLS.

Engraved, Printed & Coloured by R. Havell. 1836.

Red-headed Duck.
FULIGULA FERINA, STEPH
Male.1. Female.2.

Black Skimmer or Shearwater
RHINCOPS NIGRA, L.
Male

2

PLATE CCCXXIV.

1

3

Drawn from Nature by J. J. Audubon F.R.S. F.L.S.

Engraved, Printed & Coloured by R. Havell, 1836.

Bonapartian Gull

LARUS BONAPARTII, Swain and Rich

Male Spring Plumage 1. Female 2. Young first Autumn 3.

PLATE CCCXXV.

Drawn from Nature by J. J. Audubon FRS. F.L.S.

Engraved, Printed & Coloured by R. Havell 1836

Buffel-headed Duck.
FULIGULA ALBEOLA.
Male 1. Female 2.

PLATE CCCXXVI.

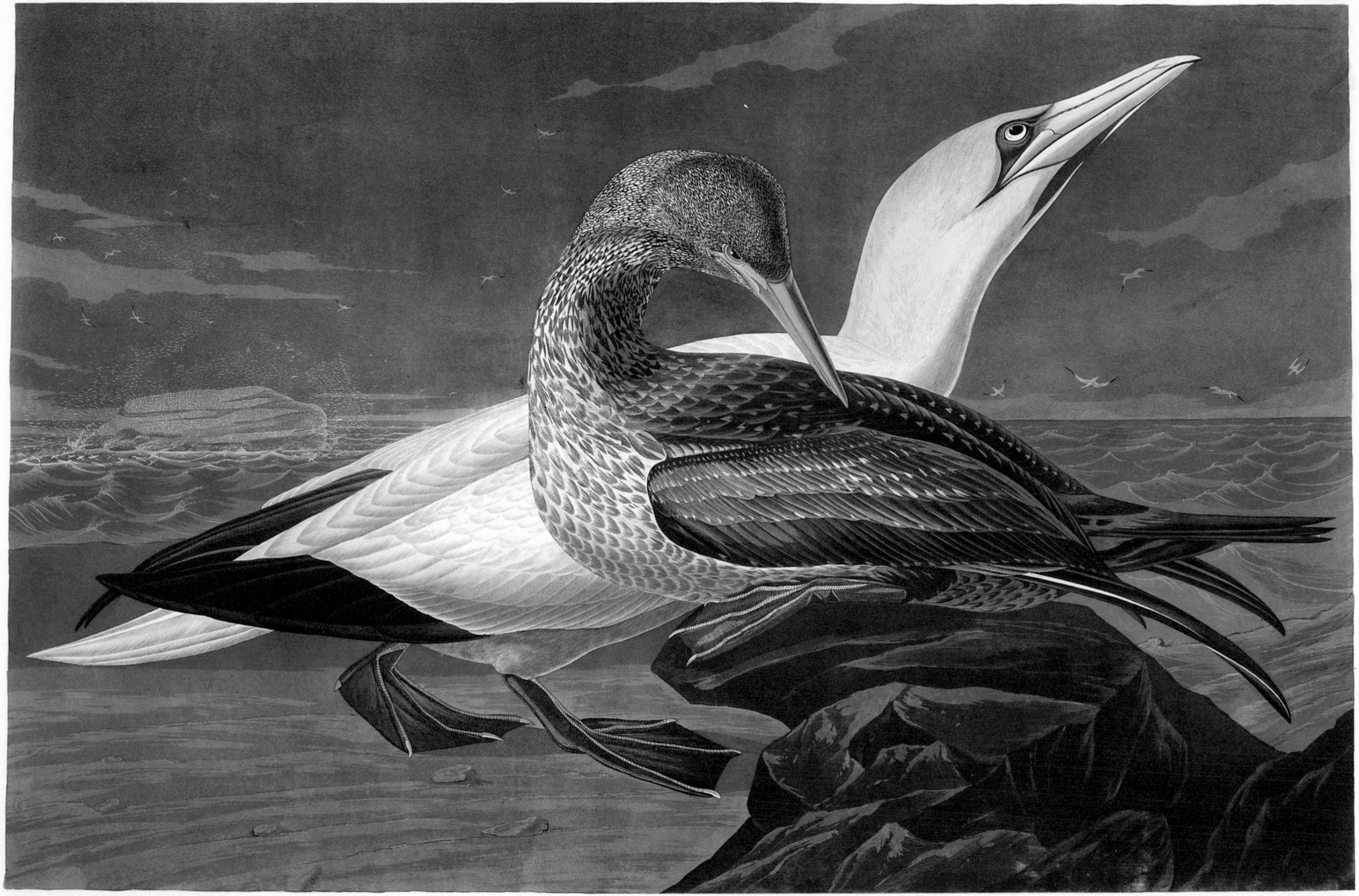

1

2

Gannet

SULA BASSANA, Lacep. Adult Male I. Young foot Winter 2.   Gannet Rock. Gulph of St. Laurence.

PLATE CCCXXVII.

Engraved, Printed and Coloured by R. Havell 1856

Shoveller Duck
ANAS CLYPEATA, L. Male 1. Female 2.

Drawn from Nature by J. J. Audubon FRS. FLS.

PLATE CCCXXVIII.

Nº 66.

Drawn from Nature by J. J. Audubon FRS. FLS.

Engraved, Printed and Coloured by R. Havell 1836

Long-legged Avocet.
HIMANTOPUS NIGRICOLLIS, VIEILL.
Male.

PLATE CCCXXIX.

Drawn from Nature by J. J. Audubon F.R.S. F.L.S.

Engraved, Printed and Coloured by R. Havell 1836

Yellow-breasted Rail.
RALLUS NOVEBORACENCIS, BONAP.
Male Adult. Spring.

PLATE CCCXXX.

N°66.

Drawn from Nature by J. J. Audubon F.R.S. F.L.S.

Engraved, Printed and Coloured by R. Havell 1836

Ring Plover.

CHARADRIUS SEMIPALMATUS,

Adult Male 1. Young in. August 2.

PLATE CCCXXXI.

1

2

Drawn from Nature by J. J. Audubon F.R.S. F.L.S.

Goosander. MERGUS MERGANSER, L. Male 1. Female 2. Cohoes Falls, State of New York.

Engraved, Printed & Coloured by R. Havell 1836.

PLATE CCCXXXII.

Drawn from Nature by J. J. Audubon F.R.S. F.L.S.

Engraved, Printed and Coloured by R. Havell. 1836

Pied Duck.

FULIGULA LABRADORA. *Male Adult 1. Female 2.*

PLATE CCCXXXIII.

Drawn from Nature by J. J. Audubon F.R.S. F.L.S.

Engraved, Printed and Coloured by R. Havell 1836

Green Heron

ARDEA VIRESCENS, L. Adult Male 1. Young in September 2.

PLATE CCCXXXIV.

Drawn from Nature by J. J. Audubon FRS. FLS.

Black-bellied Plover
CHARADRIUS HELVETICUS,
Adult Male, Spring Plumage 1. Young in Autumn. 2. Nestling 3.

Engraved, Printed and Coloured by R. Havell 1836

PLATE CCCXXXV.

Engraved, Printed and Coloured by R. Havell. 1836.

Red-breasted Snipe.
SCOLOPAX GRISEA, GM.
Spring Plumage, 1. Winter 2.

Drawn from Nature by J. J. Audubon FRS. FLS.

Yellow-Crowned Heron
ARDEA VIOLACEA, L.
Adult Male Spring Plumage, 1. Young in October, 2.

PLATE CCCXXVII.

N°68.

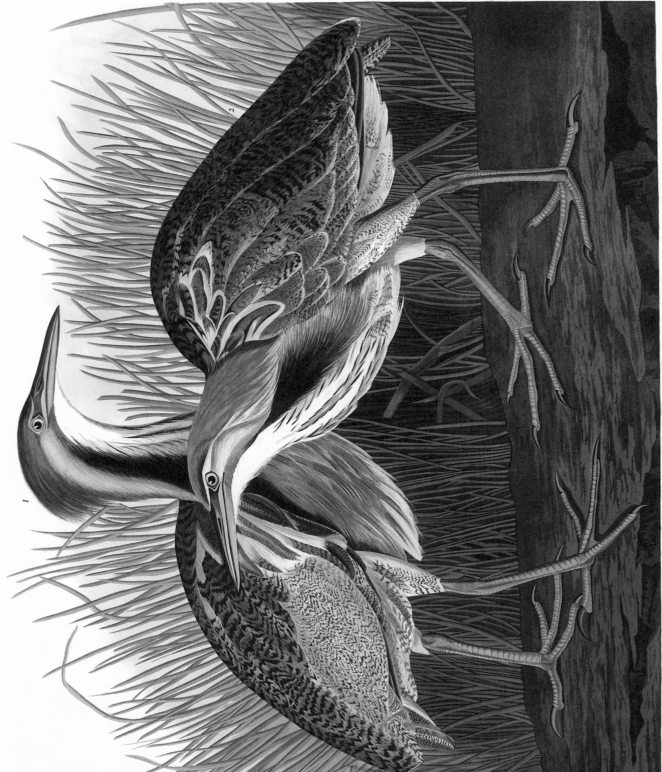

Drawn from Nature by J. J. Audubon FRS. FLS.

Engraved, Printed and Coloured by R. Havell, 1836

American Bittern
ARDEA MINOR *Male 1. Female 2.*

PLATE CCCXXXVIII.

Drawn from Nature by J.J Audubon FRS FLS.

Engraved, Printed and Coloured by R. Havell 1836.

Bemaculated Duck.
ANAS GLOCITANS Young Male in December

PLATE CCCXXIX.

Drawn from Nature by J. J. Audubon FRS. FLS.

Little Auk.
URIA ALLE, TEMM. Male 1. Female 2.

Engraved, Printed and Coloured by R. Havell, 1846

PLATE CCCXL.

Drawn from Nature by J. J. Audubon FRS. FLS.

Least Stormy-Petrel.
THALASSIDROMA PELAGICA
Male 1. Female 2.

Engraved, Printed and Coloured by R. Havell 1836.

PLATE CCCXLI.

Drawn from Nature by J. J. Audubon F.R.S. F.L.S.

Engraved, Printed and Coloured by R. Havell 1836.

Great Auk.
ALCA IMPENNIS, L.

PLATE CCCXLII.

2

Engraved, Printed and Coloured by R. Havell 1836

Golden-Eye Duck.
FULIGULA CLANGULA *Male 1. Female 2.*

Drawn from Nature by J. J. Audubon F.R.S. F.L.S

1

PLATE CCCXLIII.

Drawn from Nature by J. J. Audubon F.R.S. F.L.S.

Engraved, Printed & Coloured by R. Havell 1836.

Ruddy Duck. FULIGULA RUBIDA

Male adult 1. Female adult 2. Young Male second spring 3. Young in autumn 4.

PLATE CCXLIV.

Long-legged Sandpiper
TRINGA HIMANTOPUS
Spring Plumage, I. Winter, 2.

Drawn from Nature by J. J. Audubon F.R.S. F.L.S.

Engraved, Printed & Coloured by R. Havell 1856

PLATE CCCXLV.

Drawn from Nature by J. J. Audubon F.R.S. F.L.S.

American Widgeon
ANAS AMERICANA, Gm Male. 1. Female. 2.

Engraved, Printed & Coloured by R. Havell 1836

PLATE CCCXLVI.

Drawn from Nature by J. J. Audubon F.R.S. F.L.S.

Engraved, Printed and Coloured by R. Havell 1836

Black-Throated Diver
COLYMBUS ARCTICUS, L.   Male.1. Female. 2. Young in October. 3

PLATE CCCXLVII.

Drawn from Nature by J. J. Audubon F.R.S. F.L.S.

Engraved, Printed and Coloured by R. Havell, 1836.

Smew or White Nun

MERGUS ALBELLUS, L. *Male 1. Female 2.*

2

PLATE CCCXLVIII.

1

2

Engraved, Printed and Coloured by R. Havell, 1836.

Gadwall Duck
ANAS STREPERA, L.
Male I. Female 2.

Drawn from Nature by J.J Audubon FRS. FLS.

PLATE CCCXLIX.

2

1

Drawn from Nature by J. J. Audubon FRS FLS.

Engraved, Printed and Coloured by R. Havell 1836

Least Water-hen, Edwards

RALLUS JAMAICENSIS, Gmel

1. Male. 2. Young Adult

PLATE CCCL.

Drawn from Nature by J. J. Audubon F.R.S. F.L.S.

Engraved, Printed and Coloured by R. Havell, 1836.

Rocky Mountain Plover
CHARADRIUS MONTANUS, Townsend.
Adult Female

Great Cinereous Owl

STRIX CINEREA, —Gmelin

Female Adult.

Drawn from Nature by J. J. Audubon F.R.S. F.L.S.

Engraved, Printed and Coloured by R. Havell, 1837

Black-Winged Hawk
FALCO DISPAR, Temm
Male 1. Female 2.

Drawn from Nature by J. J. Audubon F.R.S. F.L.S.   Engraved, Printed and Coloured by R. Havell, 1837.

Chesnut-backed Titmouse *Black-capt Titmouse* *Chesnut-crowned Titmouse*

PARUS RUFESCENS, Townsend. *1. Male. 2. Female.* PARUS ATRICAPILLUS, Wils. *3. Male. 4. Female.* PARUS MINIMUS, Townsend. *5. Male. 6. Female.*
Willow Oak - *Quercus Phellœs. L.* (and Nest)

Drawn from Nature by J. J. Audubon, F.R.S. F.L.S.

Engraved, Printed and Coloured by R. Havell 1837.

Louisiana Tanager   *Scarlet Tanager*

TANAGRA LUDOVICIANA, Wils.   TANAGRA RUBRA, L.

1 & 2. Males Spring Plumage.   3. Old Male, Spring Plumage. 4. Old Female. Do., Do.

Plant, Laurus Carolinensis.

PLATE CCCLV.

Mac Gillivray's Finch
FRINGILLA MACGILLIVRAII
Male, 1. Female, 2.

Drawn from Nature by J. J. Audubon F.R.S. F.L.S.

Engraved, Printed and Coloured by R. Havell. 1837.

Drawn from Nature by J. J. Audubon F.R.S. F.L.S.

Engraved, Printed and Coloured by R. Havell, 1837.

Marsh Hawk

FALCO CYANEUS

Male Adult, 1. Female Adult, 2. Young Male, 3.

American Magpie

CORVUS PICA
Male 1. Female 2.

Drawn from Nature by J. J. Audubon F.R.S. F.L.S.

Engraved, Printed and Coloured by R. Havell. 1837.

Drawn from Nature by J. J. Audubon, F.R.S. F.L.S.

Engraved, Printed and Coloured by R. Havell, 1837.

Pine Grosbeak

PYRRHULA ENUCLEATOR
Male Adult, Spring Plumage, 1. Female, 2. Young first Winter, 3.

PLATE CCCLIX.

Arkansaw Flycatcher *Swallow-Tailed Flycatcher* *Says Flycatcher*

MUSCICAPA VERTICALIS, Bonap   MUSCICAPA FORFICATA, Gme.   MUSCICAPA SAYA, Bonap.

1. Male. 2. Female.   3. Male.   4. Male. 5. Female

Drawn from Nature by J. J. Audubon F.R.S. F.L.S.   Engraved, Printed and Coloured by R. Havell, 1857

Drawn from Nature by J. J. Audubon F.R.S. F.L.S.

Engraved, Printed and Coloured by R. Havell. 1837

Winter Wren

SYLVIA TROGLODYTES

Male, I. Female, 2. Young in Autumn, 3.

Rock Wren

TROGLODYTES OBSELATA, Say.

Female, 4

PLATE CCCLXI.

Drawn from Nature by J. J. Audubon F.R.S. F.L.S.

Engraved, Printed and Coloured by R. Havell 1837.

Long-tailed or Dusky Grous

TETRAO OBSCURUS

Male. 1. Female. 2.

1 *Yellow billed Magpie*   2 *Stellers Jay*   3 *Ultramarine Jay*   4,5 *Clark's Crow*
CORVUS NUTALLII, Aud.   CORVUS STELLERII   CORVUS ULTRAMARINUS   CORVUS COLUMBIANUS, Wils

Plant Platanus racemosus Nuttall
Acorn of Quercus macrocarpa. Mich

Drawn from Nature by J. J. Audubon F.R.S. F.L.S.

Engraved, Printed and Coloured by R. Havell. 1837

Bohemian Chatterer

Drawn from Nature by J. J. Audubon F.R.S. F.L.S.

Engraved, Printed & Coloured by R. Havell, 1837

BOMBYCILLA GARRULA *Male 1. Female 2.*
Pyrus Americanus Canadian Service Tree

White-winged Crossbill

LOXIA LEUCOPTERA Gm

Male adult, 1. 2. Female adult, 3. Young. F. 4.
New Foundland alder

Drawn from Nature by J. J. Audubon F.R.S. F.L.S.

Engraved, Printed & Coloured by R. Havell, 1837.

PLATE CCCLXV.

Drawn from Nature by J. J. Audubon FRS. FLS.

Engraved, Printed & Coloured by R. Havell 1837

Lapland Long-spur

FRINGILLA LAPONICA

Male Spring plumage 1. Male in Winter 2. Female 3.

PLATE CCCLXVI.

Drawn from Nature by J. J. Audubon F.R.S. F.L.S.

Engraved, Printed & Coloured by R. Havell 1837

Iceland or Jer Falcon

FALCO ISLANDICUS, Lath

Female Birds

PLATE CCCLXVII.

Band-tailed Pigeon 1. Male. 2. Female.

COLUMBA FASCIATA, Say
Plant Nuttall Cornel
Cornus Nuttalli. Aud

Drawn from Nature by J. J. Audubon F.R.S. F.L.S.

Engraved, Printed and Coloured by R. Havell, 1837

PLATE CCCLXVIII.

Drawn from Nature by J. J. Audubon F.R.S. F.L.S.

Engraved, Printed & Coloured by R. Havell 1837

Rock Grous

TETRAO RUPESTRIS, Leach Male in Winter 1. Female Summer Plumage 2. Young in August 3.

₁Mountain Mocking bird, Male

ORPHEUS MONTANUS, Townsend

Plant *Mistletoe*
Viscum Verticillatum

₂₃Varied Thrush, Male & Female

TURDUS NÆVIUS, Gm

Drawn from Nature by J. J. Audubon F.R.S. F.L.S.

Engraved, Printed & Coloured by R. Havell, 1837

PLATE CCCLXX.

American Water Ouzel

CINCLUS AMERICANUS *Male.*1. *Female.*2.

Drawn from Nature by J.J. Audubon FRS. FLS.

Engraved, Printed & Coloured by R. Havell 1837

PLATE CCCLXXI.

Engraved, Printed & Coloured by R. Havell 1837

Cock of the Plains

TETRAO UROPHASIANUS

Male.1. Female. 2.

Drawn from Nature by J. J. Audubon F.R.S. F.L.S.

PLATE CCCLXXII.

Drawn from Nature by J. J. Audubon F.R.S. F.L.S.

Engraved, Printed & Coloured by R. Havell, 1837

Common Buzzard
BUTEO VULGARIS
Female
Marsh Hare. Female, Lepus Palustris, Bachman

PLATE CCCLXXIII.

Evening Grosbeak
FRINGILLA VESPERTINA, Cooper
Old Male 1.

Spotted Grosbeak
FRINGILLA MACULATA
Male 2.3. Female 4.

Drawn from Nature by J. J. Audubon F.R.S. F.L.S.

Engraved, Printed & Coloured by R. Havell. 1837

Sharp-shinned Hawk
FALCO VELOX, Wilson *Male* 1. *Female* 2.

PLATE CCCLXXV.

Lesser Red-Poll

FRINGILLA LINARIA, L

Male 1. Female 2.

Plant Snow Berry

Symphoricarpos Racemosus

Drawn from Nature by J. J. Audubon F.R.S. F.L.S.

Engraved, Printed & Coloured by R. Havell, 1837

PLATE CCCLXXVI.

Drawn from Nature by J J Audubon FRS. FLS.

Engraved Printed & Coloured by R Havell 1837

Trumpeter Swan
CYGNUS BUCCINATOR *Young*

PLATE CCCLXVII.

Drawn from Nature by J. J. Audubon FRS. FLS.

Scolopaceus Courlan

ARAMUS SCOLOPACEUS, Viell

Engraved, Printed and Coloured by R. Havell 1837

Hawk Owl

STRIX FUNEREA

Male 1. Female 2.

Drawn from Nature by J. J. Audubon F.R.S. F.L.S.

Engraved, Printed and Coloured by R. Havell, 1837.

PLATE CCCLXXIX.

Ruff-necked Humming-bird

TROCHILUS RUFUS, Latham
1. 2. Males 3. Female & Nest.
Plant Cleome heptaphylla

Drawn from Nature by J. J. Audubon F.R.S. F.L.S.

Engraved, Printed & Coloured by R. Havell, 1837.

PLATE CCCLXXX.

Tengmalm's Owl

STRIX TENGMALMI

Male 1. Female 2.

Drawn from Nature by J. J. Audubon F.R.S. F.L.S.

Engraved, Printed and Coloured by R. Havell, 1837.

PLATE CCCLXXXI.

Drawn from Nature by J J Audubon F.R.S. F.L.S.

1

2

Engraved, Printed and Coloured by R. Havell 1837.

Snow Goose

ANSER HYPERBOREUS, Pallas.

Adult Male 1 Young Female, foot Winter 2.

PLATE CCCLXXII.

Drawn from Nature by J. J. Audubon F.R.S. F.L.S.

Engraved, Printed and Coloured by R. Havell 1837

Sharp-tailed Grous

TETRAO PHASIANELLUS *Male 1. Female 2.*

2   1

PLATE CCCLXXXIII.

Long-eared Owl
STRIX OTUS
Male

Drawn from Nature by J. J. Audubon F.R.S. F.L.S.

Engraved, Printed & Coloured by R. Havell, 1837

PLATE CCCLXXXIV.

Drawn from Nature by J. J. Audubon F.R.S. F.L.S.

Black-throated Bunting

FRINGILLA AMERICANA
Male 1. Female 2.

Engraved, Printed & Coloured by R. Havell, 1837.

PLATE CCCLXXXV.

Drawn from Nature by J. J. Audubon F.R.S. F.L.S.

Engraved, Printed & Coloured by R. Havell, 1857.

Bank Swallow   *Violet-Green Swallow*

HIRUNDO RIPARIA   HIRUNDO THALASSINUS, Swain

Male 1. Female 2. Young 3.   Male 4. Female 5.

PLATE CCCLXXVI.

White Heron

ARDEA ALBA, Linn. *Male, Spring Plumage*

Horned Agama

Tapayaxin of Hernandez

Drawn from Nature by J. J. Audubon F.R.S. F.L.S.

N.º 76.

PLATE CCCLXXXVII.

Drawn from Nature by J J Audubon FRS. FLS.

Glossy Ibis
IBIS FALCINELLUS Male Adult

Engraved, Printed and Coloured by R Havell 1837

PLATE CCCLXXXVIII.

Nuttall's Starling   *Yellow-headed Troopial*   *Bullock's Oriole*

ICTERUS TRICOLOR, Aud   ICTERUS XANTHOCEPHALUS, Bonap   ICTERUS BULLOCKII
1. Adult Male   *2. Adult Male 3. Do. Female 4. head of Young Male*   *5. Adult Male*

Drawn from Nature by J. J. Audubon F.R.S. F.L.S.   Engraved, Printed & Coloured by R. Havell, 1837

PLATE CCCLXXXIX.

Drawn from Nature by J. J. Audubon F.R.S. F.L.S.

Engraved, Printed & Coloured by R. Havell, 1837

Red-Cockaded Woodpecker

PICUS QUERULUS, Wils

Males 1. Female 2.

Drawn from Nature by J. J. Audubon F.R.S. F.L.S.

Engraved, Printed & Coloured by R. Havell, 1837

Lark Finch

FRINGILLA GRAMMACA, Say
Male. I.

Prairie Finch

FRINGILLA BICOLOR, Townsend
2. Male. 3. Female.

Brown Song Sparrow

FRINGILLA CINEREA, Gmel
4. Male.

PLATE CCCXCI.

Brant Goose
ANSER BERNICLA
1 Male. 2 Female.

Drawn from Nature by J. J. Audubon F.R.S. F.L.S.

Engraved, Printed and Coloured by R. Havell. 1837

PLATE CCCXCII.

Engraved, Printed and Coloured by R. Havell, 1837

Louisiana Hawk.

BUTEO HARRISI, Aud.

Adult Female

Drawn from Nature by J. J. Audubon F.R.S. F.L.S.

PLATE CCCXCIII.

Drawn from Nature by J. J. Audubon F.R.S. F.L.S.

Engraved, Printed & Coloured by R. Havell, 1837

Townsend's Warbler

SYLVIA TOWNSENDI, Nuttall
1. Male

Arctic Blue-bird

SIALIA ARCTICA, Swain
2. Male 3. Female
Plant { Carolina Allspice
CALYCANTHUS FLORIDUS

Western Blue-bird

SIALIA OCCIDENTALIS, Townsend
4. Male 5. Female

Drawn from Nature by J. J. Audubon F.R.S. F.L.S.

Engraved, Printed & Coloured by R. Havell, 1837

Chestnut-coloured Finch   Black-headed Siskin Black crown Bunting Lath *Arctic Ground Finch*

PLECTROPHANES ORNATA, Towns   FRINGILLA MAGELLANICA, Viell   EMBERIZA ATRICAPILLA, Gmel   PIPILO ARCTICA, Swain

1. Male. Spring   *2. Old Male*   *3. Adult Male*   *4. Male. 5. Female*

PLATE CCCXCV.

Drawn from Nature by J. J. Audubon F.R.S. F.L.S.

Engraved, Printed & Coloured by R. Havell, 1837.

Audubon's Warbler

SYLVIA AUDUBONI, Townsend
1. Male. 2. Female.

Hermit Warbler

SYLVIA OCCIDENTALIS, Townsend
3. Male. 4. Female.
Plant. Strawberry Tree
EUYONUMUS AMÉRICANA

Black-throated gray Warbler

SYLVIA NIGRESCENS, Townsend
5 and 6. Males.

PLATE CCCXCVI.

Engraved, Printed and Coloured by R. Havell 1837.

Burgomaster Gull

LARUS GLAUCUS, Brunnich   1. Adult Male. 2. Young, first Autumn.

Drawn from Nature by J.J. Audubon F.R.S. F.L.S.

PLATE CCCXCVII.

Drawn from Nature by J J Audubon F.R.S. F.L.S.

Engraved, Printed and Coloured by R. Havell 1837

Scarlet Ibis

IBIS RUBRA, Viell

1 Adult Male 2 Young Second Autumn

Drawn from Nature by J. J. Audubon F.R.S. F.L.S.

Engraved, Printed & Coloured by R. Havell, 1837

Lazuli Finch

FRINGILLA AMŒNA

1. Male Spring Plumange.

Clay-Coloured Finch

FRINGILLA PALLIDA, Swains *2. Male.*

Plant Liberty Bush AZALEA NUDIFLORA

Oregon Snow Finch

FRINGILLA OREGONA, Towns

3. Male. 4. Female.

Drawn from Nature by J. J. Audubon F.R.S. F.L.S.

Engraved, Printed & Coloured by R. Havell, 1837

Black-throated green Warbler
SYLVIA VIRENS
1. Male. 2. Female.

Blackburnian w.
SYLVIA BLACKBURNIÆ
3. Female.

Mourning Warbler
SYLVIA PHILADELPHIA
4. Male. 5. Female.

Drawn from Nature by J. J. Audubon F.R.S. F.L.S.

Engraved, Printed & Coloured by R. Havell, 1837

Arkansaw Siskin *Mealy Red-poll* *Louisiana Tanager* *Townsend's Finch* *Buff-breasted Finch*

FRINGILLA SPALTRIA LINOTA BOREALIS TANAGRA LUDOVICIANA EMBERIZA TOWNSENDI EMBERIZA PICTA

1. Male 2. Male 3. Female 4. Male 5. Male

PLATE CCCCI.

N° 81.

2

1

Red-breasted Merganser
MERGUS SERRATOR, L.
Male. 1. Female. 2.
Plant Sarracenia flava.

Drawn from Nature by J.J. Audubon F.R.S. F.L.S.

Engraved, Printed and Coloured by Rob. Havell 1838

PLATE CCCCII.

Drawn from Nature by J.J Audubon FRS. FLS.   1   2   3   4   5   Engraved, Printed and Coloured by Robt. Havell 1838

Black-throated Guillemot   *Notted-billed Auk*   *Curled-Crested Auk*   *Horned-billed Guillemot*

MERGULUS ANTIQUUS, Bonap 1. Adult. 2. Young.   PHALERIS NODIROSTRIS, Bonap   PHALERIS SUPERCILIATA, Bonap   CERATORRHINA OCCIDENTALIS, Bonap

PLATE CCCCIII.

Drawn from Nature by J. J. Audubon FRS. FLS.

Engraved, Printed & Coloured by Robt. Havell 1838

Golden-eye Duck.
CLANGULA VULGARIS
Male, Summer Plumage

PLATE CCCCIV.

Drawn from Nature by J. J. Audubon FRS FLS

Engraved, Printed & Coloured by Robt. Havell 1838

Eared Grebe.
PODICEPS AURITUS
1. Adult. 2. Young foot Winter.

PLATE CCCCV.

N°81.

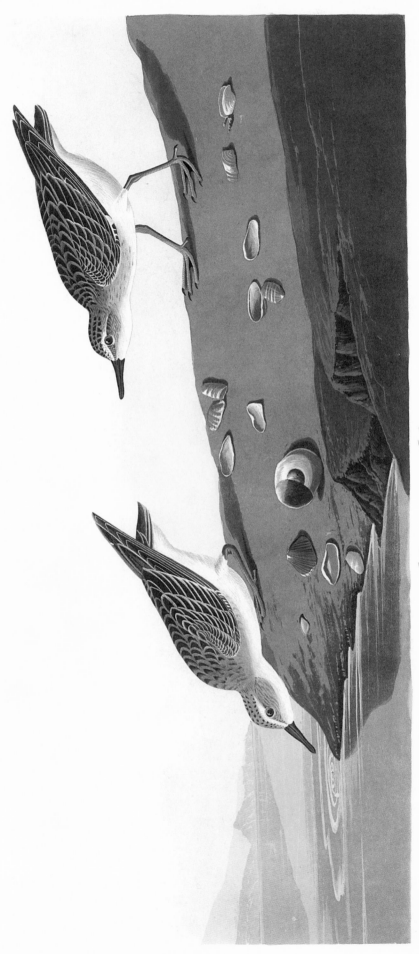

Semipalmated Sandpiper
TRINGA SEMIPALMATA, Wils

Drawn from Nature by J. J. Audubon FRS. F.L.S.

Engraved, Printed & Coloured by Robt. Havell 1838

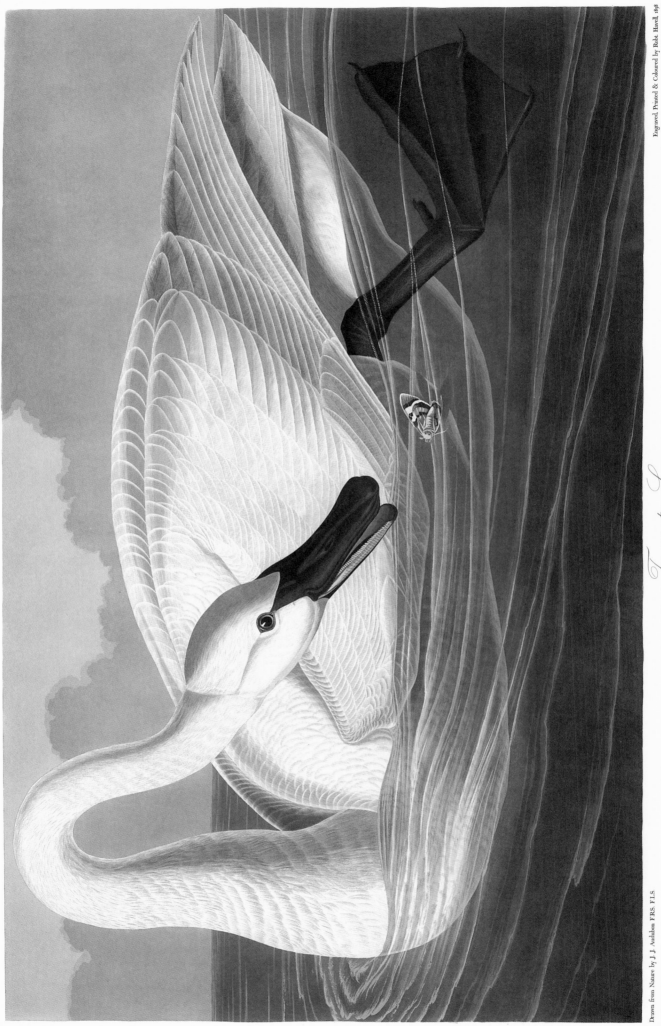

Engraved, Printed & Coloured by Robt. Havell 1838

Trumpeter Swan
CYGNUS BUCCINATOR. Richardson.
Adult.

Drawn from Nature by J.J. Audubon FRS. FLS

PLATE CCCCVII.

Drawn from Nature by J. J. Audubon F.R.S. F.L.S.

Engraved, Printed and Coloured by Robt. Havell 1838

Dusky Albatros
DIOMEDEA FUSCA

PLATE CCCCVIII.

Drawn from Nature by J J Audubon FRS. F.L.S.

American Scoter Duck
FLIGULA AMERICANA
Male 1. Female 2.

Engraved, Printed and Coloured by Robt. Havell 1838

PLATE CCCCIX.

Drawn from Nature by J. J. Audubon F.R.S. F.L.S.

Engraved, Printed and Coloured by Robt. Havell 1848

Havell's Tern. 1.
STERNA HAVELLI, Aud

Trudeau's Tern. 2.
STERNA TRUDEAUI, Aud

PLATE CCCCX.

Drawn from Nature by J. J. Audubon F.R.S. F.L.S.

Marsh Tern

Engraved, Printed and Coloured by Robt. Havell, 1838

STERNA ANGLICA, Montagu *Male, Summer Plumage.*

PLATE CCCXL.

Common American Swan
CYGNUS AMERICANUS, Sharpless
Nymphea flava - Leitner

Drawn from Nature by J. J. Audubon F.R.S. F.L.S.

PLATE CCCCXII.

Drawn from Nature by J. J. Audubon FRS. FLS.

Violet-green Cormorant   *Townsend's Cormorant*

PHALACROCORAX RESPLENDENS, Aud Female in Winter   PHALACROCORAX TOWNSENDI, Aud Male

Engraved, Printed and Coloured by Robt. Havell 1838

PLATE CCCXIII.

Nº 83.

Californian Partridge
PERDIX CALIFORNICA, Lath. *Male 1. Female 2.*

Drawn from Nature by J. J. Audubon F.R.S. F.L.S.

Engraved, Printed & Coloured by Robt. Havell, 1838

Golden-winged Warbler *Cape May Warbler*
SYLVIA CHRYSOPTERA, Lath   SYLVIA MARITIMA, Wils
Male 1. Female 2.   *Male 3. Female 4.*

Drawn from Nature by J. J. Audubon F.R.S. F.L.S.

Engraved, Printed & Coloured by Robt. Havell. 1838.

Brown Creeper

CERTHIA FAMILIARIS, Lin
Male 1. Female 2.

Californian Nuthatch

SITTA PYGMEA, Vig
3. 4.

PLATE CCCCXVI.

Drawn from Nature by J. J. Audubon F.R.S. F.L.S.

Engraved, Printed & Coloured by Robt. Havell, 1838.

Hairy Woodpecker   Red-bellied Woodpecker   Red-shafted Woodpecker   Lewis' Woodpecker   Red-breasted Woodpecker

PICUS VILLOSUS, Linn.   PICUS CAROLINUS, Linn.   PICUS MEXICANUS, Aud.   PICUS TORQUATUS, Wils.   PICUS RUBER, Lath.

1. Male. 2. Female.   3. Male. 4. Female.   5. Male. 6. Female.   7. Male. 8. Female.   9. Male. 10. Female.

PLATE CCCCXVII.

Drawn from Nature by J. J. Audubon F.R.S. F.L.S.

Engraved, Printed and Coloured by Robt. Havell, 1838.

Maria's Woodpecker Three-toed Woodpecker Phillips' Woodpecker Canadian Woodpecker Harris's Woodpecker Audubon's Woodpecker

PICUS MARTINI, Aud	PICUS HIRSITUS, Vieil	PICUS PHILLIPSI, Aud	PICUS CANADENSIS, Buff	PICUS HARRISI, Aud	PICUS AUDUBONI, Trudeau.
1.Male. 2.Female.	3.Male. 4.Female.	5. and 6.Males.	7.Male	8.Male. 9.Female.	10.Male.

PLATE CCCCXVIII.

Drawn from Nature by J. J. Audubon FRS. F.L.S.

Engraved, Printed & Coloured by Robt. Havell 1838.

American Ptarmigan

TETRAO MUTUS, Leach
1. *Male Spring Plumamge*

White-tailed Grous

Tetrao leucurus, Swains
2. *Winter Plumange*

PLATE CCCCXIX.

Drawn from Nature by J. J. Audubon F.R.S. F.L.S.

Engraved, Printed & Coloured by Robt. Havell, 1838

Little Tawny Thrush

TURDUS MINOR, Gm
1. Male.

Ptiliogony's Townsendi, Aud

2. Female.

Canada Jay

CORVUS CANADENSIS, Linn
3. Young, Male.

Drawn from Nature by J. J. Audubon F.R.S. F.L.S.

Engraved, Printed and Coloured by Robt. Havell 1838

Prairie Starling

ICTERUS GUBERNATOR, Aud
Male. 1. Female. 2.

PLATE CCCCXXI.

Engraved, Printed and Coloured by Robt. Havell 1838

Brown Pelican
PELICANUS FUSCUS
Young first Winter

Drawn from Nature by J. J. Audubon FRS FLS

Nº 85.

Drawn from Nature by J. J. Audubon F.R.S. F.L.S.

Engraved, Printed and Coloured by Robt. Havell, 1838

Rough-legged Falcon
BUTEO LAGOPUS
1. Old Male. 2. Young first Winter.

PLATE CCCCXXIII.

Drawn from Nature by J. J. Audubon F.RS. F.L.S.

Engraved, Printed & Coloured by Robt. Havell 1838

Plumed Partridge
PERDIX PLUMIFERA, Gould 2.Male 3.Female

Thick-legged Partridge
PERDIX NEOXENUS, Aud 1.Supposed Young Male.

2

1

3

Drawn from Nature by J. J. Audubon F.R.S. F.L.S.

Engraved, Printed & Coloured by Robt. Havell, 1838

Lazuli Finch

FRINGILLA AMŒNA, Say

1. Female

Cow-pen Bird

ICTERUS PECORIS, Bonap

4. Young Male

Crimson-necked Bull-finch

PYRRHULA FRONTALIS, Bonap

2. Male

Evening Grosbeak

FRINGILLA VESPERTINA, Cooper

5. Female 6. Young Male

Grey-crowned Linnet

LINARIA TEPHROCOTIS, Swains

3. Male

Brown Longspur

PLECTROPHANES TOWNSENDI, Aud

7. Female

Columbian Humming Bird

TROCHILUS ANNA, Lesson
1. 2. 3. 4. Male. 5. Female and Nest.
Plant Hibiscus Virginicus.

Drawn from Nature by J. J. Audubon F.R.S. F.L.S.

Engraved, Printed & Coloured by Robt. Havell. 1838

Drawn from Nature by J. J. Audubon F.R.S. F.L.S.

Engraved, Printed and Coloured by Robt. Havell, 1838

Californian Vulture

CATHARTES CALIFORNIANUS, Illiger
Old Male

PLATE CCCCXXVII.

Drawn from Nature by J. J. Audubon FRS FLS.   *White-legged Oyster-catcher*   *Slender-billed Oyster-catcher*   Engraved, Printed and Coloured by Robt. Havell, 1838

1   2

HŒMATOPUS BACHMANI, Aud. 1.Male   HŒMATOPUS TOWNSENDI, Aud. 2.Female

Townsend's Sandpiper

FRINCA TOWNSENDI, Aud
Females

PLATE CCCCXXIX.

Engraved, Printed & Coloured by Robt. Havell 1838

Western Duck

FULIGULA STELLERI, Bonap

Drawn from Nature by J. J. Audubon FRS. FLS.

PLATE CCCCXXX

Drawn from Nature by J. J. Audubon F.R.S. F.L.S.

Engraved, Printed & Coloured by Robt. Havell 1838.

Slender-billed Guillemot
URIA TOWNSENDI, Aud
1 Male. 2 Female.

Drawn from Nature by J. J. Audubon F.R.S. F.L.S.

Engraved, Printed & Coloured by Robt. Havell, 1838.

American Flamingo

PHŒNICOPTERUS RUBER, Linn.
Old Male.

1.—Profile view of Bill at its greatest extension.
2.—Superior front view of upper Mandible.
3.—Interior front view of upper Mandible.
4.—Inferior front view of lower Mandible.
5.—Interior front view of lower Mandible with the tongue in.

6.—Profile view of Tongue.
7.—Superior front view of Tongue.
8.—Inferior front view of Tongue.
9.—Perpendicular front view of the foot fully expanded.

PLATE CCCCXXXII.

Nº 87.

Drawn from Nature by J. J. Audubon FRS. FLS.

Engraved, Printed & Coloured by Robt. Havell. 1838

Burrowing Owl
STRIX CUNICULARIA
1. Male.

Large-headed Burrowing Owl
STRIX CALIFORNICA
2. Male.

Little night Owl
STRIX NOCTUA, Lath.
3. Female.

Columbian Owl
STRIX PASSERINOIDES, Temm.
4.5. Male.

Short-eared Owl
STRIX BRACHYOTUS, Wils.
6. Male.

PLATE CCCCXXXIII.

Drawn from Nature by J. J. Audubon F.R.S. F.L.S.

Engraved, Printed & Coloured by Robt. Havell, 1838

Bullock's Oriole
ICTERUS BULLOCKI, Swains
1. Young Male 2. Old Female

Baltimore Oriole
ICTERUS BALTIMORE, Bonap
3. Old Female

Mexican Goldfinch
CARDUELLIS MEXICANUS, Swains
4. Male 5. Female

Varied Thrush
TURDUS NŒVIUS, Lath
6. Female

Common Water Thrush
TURDUS AQUATICUS, Wilson
7. Male

PLATE CCCCXXXIV.

Drawn from Nature by J. J. Audubon F.R.S. F.L.S.

Engraved, Printed & Coloured by Robt. Havell, 1838.

Little Tyrant Fly-catcher
TYRANNULA PUSILLA, Swains

Blue Mountain Warbler
SYLVIA MONTANA, Wilson
3. Male

Short-legged Pewee
MUSCICAPA PHŒBE, Lath
5. Male

Small-headed Fly-catcher
MUSCICAPA MINUTA, Wils
Male 2.

Bartram's Vireo
VIREO BARTRAMI, Swains
4. Male

Rocky Mountain Fly-catcher
TYRANNULA NIGRICANS, Swains
6. Male

Drawn from Nature by J. J. Audubon F.R.S. F.L.S.

Engraved, Printed & Coloured by Robt. Havell, 1838

Columbian Water Ouzel
CINCLUS TOWNSENDI, Aud
1. Female.

Arctic Water Ouzel
CINCLUS MORTONI, Townsend
2. Male.

Plate Information

The information below is as follows: the common and scientific species names as given by Audubon, followed by the current common and scientific species names and then the size of each plate in inches. The numbering of the plates is as it was originally.

PLATE NUMBER
Audubon common name
Audubon species name
Current common name
Current species name
Original plate size (inches)

PLATE I
Wild turkey (male)
Meleagris gallopavo
Wild turkey
Meleagris gallopavo
38 ⅛ x 25 ½

PLATE II
Yellow-billed cuckoo
Coccyzus carolinensis
Yellow-billed cuckoo
Coccyzus americanus
20 ⅞ x 26 ⅜

PLATE III
Prothonotary warbler
Dacnis protonotarius
Prothonotary warbler
Protonotaria citrea
20 ½ x 12 ½

PLATE IV
Purple finch
Fringilla purpurea
Purple finch
Carpodacus purpureus
20 ⅜ x 12 ½

PLATE V
Bonaparte fly catcher
Muscicapa bonapartii
Canada warbler
Wilsonia canadensis
20 ½ x 12 ½

PLATE VI
Wild turkey (female)
Meleagris gallopavo
Wild turkey
Meleagris gallopavo
25 ⅝ x 38 ¼

PLATE VII
Purple grackle
Quiscalus versicolor
Common grackle
Quiscalus quiscula
26 ⅜ x 20 ¾

PLATE VIII
White throated sparrow
Fringilla pensylvanica
White-throated sparrow
Zonotrichia albicollis
20 ½ x 12 ¾

PLATE IX
Selby's fly catcher
Muscicapa selbii
Hooded warbler
Wilsonia citrina
20 ¾ x 12 ⅞

PLATE X
Brown lark
Anthus aquaticus
Water pipit
Anthus spinoletta
12 ¾ x 20 ½

PLATE 11
The bird of Washington or great American sea eagle
Falco washingtoniensis
Bald eagle
Haliæetus leucocephalus
38 ¼ x 25 ⅝

PLATE 12
Baltimore oriole
Icterus baltimore
Baltimore oriole
Icterus galbula
26 x 23 ¾

PLATE 13
Snow bird
Fringilla nivalis
Dark-eyed junco
Junco hyemalis
19 ⅜ x 12 ¼

PLATE 14
Prairie warbler
Sylvia discolor
Prairie warbler
Dendroica discolor
19 ⅝ x 12 ½

PLATE XV
Blue yellow back warbler
Sylvia americana
Northern parula
Parula americana
19 ¼ x 12 ¼

PLATE 16
Great footed hawk
Falco peregrinus
Peregrine falcon
Falco peregrinus
25 ⅝ x 38 ¼

PLATE 17
Carolina pigeon or turtle dove
Columba carolinensis
Mourning dove
Zenaida macroura
26 ¾ x 20 ¾

PLATE 18
Bewick's long tailed wren
Troglodytes bewickii
Bewick's wren
Thryomanes bewickii
19 ⅝ x 12 ⅛

PLATE 19
Louisiana water thrush
Turdus aquaticus
Louisiana waterthrush
Seiurus motacilla
19 ¾ x 12 ½

PLATE 20
Blue winged yellow warbler
Dacnis solitaria
Blue-winged warbler
Vermivora pinus
19 ½ x 12 ¼

PLATE 21
The mocking bird
Turdus polyglottus
Northern mockingbird
Mimus polyglottos
33 ¼ x 23 ⅝

PLATE 22
Purple martin
Hirundo purpurea
Purple martin
Progne subis
25 ½ x 20 ½

PLATE 23
Maryland yellow throat
Sylvia trichas
Common yellowthroat
Geothlypis trichas
19 ⅜ x 12 ⅛

PLATE 24
Roscœ's yellow throat
Sylvia rosco
Common yellowthroat
Geothlypis trichas
19 ⅝ x 12 ¼

PLATE 25
Song sparrow
Fringilla melodia
Song sparrow
Melospiza melodia
19 ⅜ x 12 ⅛

PLATE 26
Carolina parrot
Psitacus carolinensis
Carolina parakeet
Conuropsis carolinensis
33 ¼ x 24

PLATE 27
Red headed woodpecker
Picus erythrocephalus
Red-headed woodpecker
Melanerpes erythrocephalus
25 ⅜ x 21 ¾

PLATE 28
Solitary flycatcher
Vireo solitarius
Blue-headed vireo
Vireo solitarius
19 ½ x 12 ¼

PLATE 29
Towee bunting
Fringilla erythropthalma
Eastern towhee
Pipilo erythrophthalmus
19 ⅝ x 12 ⅜

PLATE 30
Vigors vireo
Vireo vigorsii
Pine warbler
Dendroica pinus
19 ½ x 12 ¼

PLATE 31
White-headed eagle
Falco leucocephalus
Bald eagle
Haliæetus leucocephalus
25 ⅝ x 38 ¼

PLATE 32
Black-billed cuckoo
Coccyzus erythrophthalmus
Black-billed cuckoo
Coccyzus erythropthalmus
18 ¾ x 26 ⅜

PLATE 33
Yellow bird or American goldfinch
Carduelis americana
American goldfinch
Carduelis tristis
19 ⅜ x 12 ¼

PLATE 34
Worm-eating warbler
Dacnis vermivora
Worm-eating warbler
Helmitheros vermivorum
19 ⅝ x 12 ¼

PLATE 35
Children's warbler
Silvia childreni
Yellow warbler
Dendroica petechia
19 ½ x 12 ¼

PLATE 36
Stanley hawk
Astur stanleii
Cooper's hawk
Accipiter cooperii
38 ¼ x 25 ⅝

PLATE 37
Gold-winged woodpecker
Picus auratus
Northern flicker
Colaptes auratus
25 ⅞ x 20 ¾

PLATE 38
Kentucky warbler
Sylvia formosa
Kentucky warbler
Oporornis formosus
19 ½ x 12 ¼

PLATE 39
Crested titmouse
Parus bicolor
Tufted titmouse
Parus bicolor
19 ½ x 12 ¼

PLATE 40
American redstart
Muscicapa ruticilla
American redstart
Setophaga ruticilla
19 ⅜ x 12 ⅛

PLATE 41
Ruffed grous
Tetrao umbellus
Ruffed grouse
Bonasa umbellus
25 ⅝ x 38 ¼

PLATE 42
Orchard oriole
Icterus spurius
Orchard oriole
Icterus spurius
26 x 20 ⅞

PLATE 43
Cedar bird
Bombycilla carolinensis
Cedar waxwing
Bombycilla cedrorum
19 ⅝ x 12 ¼

PLATE 44
Summer red bird
Tanagra æstiva
Summer tanager
Piranga rubra
19 ⅝ x 12 ¼

PLATE 45
Traill's fly-catcher
Muscicapa trailli
Willow flycatcher
Empidonax traillii
19 ½ x 12 ¼

PLATE 46
Barred owl
Strix nebulosa
Barred owl
Strix varia
38 ¼ x 25 ⅝

PLATE 47
Ruby-throated humming bird
Trochilus colubris
Ruby-throated hummingbird
Archilochus colubris
25 ⅞ x 20 ¾

PLATE 48
Cerulean warbler
Sylvia azurea
Cerulean warbler
Dendroica cerulea
19 ¾ x 12 ¼

PLATE 49
Blue-green warbler
Sylvia rara
Cerulean warbler
Dendroica cerulea
19 ⅝ x 12 ¼

PLATE 50
Swainson's warbler
Sylvicola swainsonia
Magnolia warbler
Dendroica magnolia
19 ½ x 12 ¼

PLATE 51
Red tailed hawk
Falco borealis
Red-tailed hawk
Buteo jamaicensis
38 ⅛ x 25 ½

PLATE 52
Chuck will's widow
Caprimulgus carolinesis
Chuck-will's widow
Caprimulgus carolinensis
26 x 20 ⅝

PLATE 53
Painted bunting
Fringilla ciris
Painted bunting
Passerina ciris
19 ⅜ x 12 ⅛

PLATE 54
Rice bunting
Icterus agripennis
Bobolink
Dolichonyx oryzivorus
19 ½ x 12 ¼

PLATE 55
Cuvier's wren
Regulus cuvieri
Cuvier's kinglet
Regulus cuvieri
19 ½ x 12 ⅛

PLATE 56
Red-shouldered hawk
Falco lineatus
Red-shouldered hawk
Buteo lineatus
38 ⅛ x 25 ½

PLATE 57
Loggerhead shrike
Lanius carolinensis
Loggerhead shrike
Lanius ludovicianus
26 x 20 ⅝

PLATE 58
Hermit thrush
Turdus solitarius
Hermit thrush
Catharus guttatus
19 ⅜ x 12 ⅛

PLATE 59
Chesnut sided warbler
Sylvia Icterocephala
Chestnut-sided warbler
Dendroica pensylvanica
19 ½ x 12 ¼

PLATE 60
Carbonated warbler
Sylvia carbonata
Carbonated warbler
Sylvia carbonata
19 ½ x 12 ¼

PLATE 61
Great horned-owl
Strix virginiana
Great horned owl
Bubo virginianus
38 ⅛ x 25 ½

PLATE 62
Pafsenger pigeon
Columba migratoria
Passenger pigeon
Ectopistes migratorius
26 x 20 ⅞

PLATE 63
White eyed flycatcher
Vireo noveboracensis
White-eyed vireo
Vireo griseus
19 ⅜ x 12 ¼

PLATE 64
Swamp sparrow
Spiza palustris
Swamp sparrow
Melospiza georgiana
19 ⅜ x 12 ¼

PLATE 65
Rathbone's warbler
Sylvia rathboni
Yellow warbler
Dendroica petechia
19 ¼ x 12 ⅛

PLATE 66
Ivory-billed woodpecker
Picus principalis
Ivory-billed woodpecker
Campephilus principalis
38 ¼ x 25 ⅝

PLATE 67
Red-winged starling
Icterus phœniceus
Red-winged blackbird
Agelaius phœniceus
25 ⅞ x 20 ¾

PLATE 68
Republican cliff swallow
Hirundo fulva
Cliff swallow
Petrochelidon pyrrhonota
19 ½ x 12 ¼

PLATE 69
Bay breasted warbler
Sylvia castanea
Bay-breasted warbler
Dendroica castanea
19 ½ x 12 ¼

PLATE 70
Henslow's bunting
Ammodramus henslowii
Henslow's sparrow
Ammodramus henslowii
19 ½ x 12 ¼

PLATE 71
Winter hawk
Circus hyemalis
Red-shouldered hawk
Buteo lineatus
25 ½ x 38 ⅛

PLATE 72
Swallow-tailed hawk
Falco furcatus
Swallow-tailed kite
Elanoides forficatus
20 ¾ x 27 ⅛

PLATE 73
Wood thrush
Turdus mustelinus
Wood thrush
Hylocichla mustelina
19 ½ x 12 ¼

PLATE 74
Indigo-bird
Fringilla cyanea
Indigo bunting
Passerina cyanea
19 ⅝ x 12 ¼

PLATE 75
Le petit caporal
Falco temerarius
Merlin
Falco columbarius
19 ½ x 12 ¼

PLATE 76
Virginian partridge
Perdix virginiana
Northern bobwhite (also red-shouldered hawk)
Colinus virginianus (also *Buteo lineatus*)
25 ⅝ x 38 ¼

PLATE 77
Belted kingfisher
Alcedo alcyon
Belted kingfisher
Megaceryle alcyon
25 ⅞ x 20 ¾

PLATE 78
Great carolina wren
Troglodytes ludovicianus
Carolina wren
Thryothorus ludovicianus
19 ¾ x 12 ⅛

PLATE 79
Tyrant flycatcher
Muscicapa tyrannus
Eastern kingbird
Tyrannus tyrannus
19 ½ x 12 ¼

PLATE 80
Anthus hypogeus
Phlox subulata
Water pipit
Anthus spinoletta
12 ¼ x 19 ⅜

PLATE 81
Fish hawk
Falco haliætus
Osprey
Pandion haliætus
38 ¼ x 25 ⅝

PLATE 82
Whip-poor-will
Caprimulgus vociferus
Whip-poor-will
Caprimulgus vociferus
25 ⅜ x 20 ¾

PLATE 83
House wren
Troglodytes œdon
House wren
Troglodytes œdon
19 ½ x 12 ¼

PLATE 84
Blue grey flycatcher
Sylvia cærula
Blue-grey gnatcatcher
Polioptila cærulea
19 ½ x 12 ¼

PLATE 85
Yellow throat warbler
Sylvia pensilis
Yellow-throated warbler
Dendroica dominica
19 ⅜ x 12 ¼

PLATE 86
Black warrior
Falco harlani
Red-tailed hawk
Buteo jamaicensis
38 ¼ x 25 ½

PLATE 87
Florida jay
Garrulus floridanus
Florida scrub jay
Aphelocoma cærulescens
25 ¾ x 20 ½

PLATE 88
Autumnal warbler
Sylvia autumnalis
Bay-breasted warbler
Dendroica castanea
19 ⅜ x 12 ¼

PLATE 89
Nashville warbler
Sylvia rubricapilla
Nashville warbler
Vermivora ruficapilla
19 ⅜ x 12 ¼

PLATE 90
Black and white creeper
Sylvia varia
Black-and-white warbler
Mniotilta varia
19 ½ x 12 ¼

PLATE 91
Broad-winged hawk
Falco pennsylvanicus
Broad-winged hawk
Buteo platypterus
38 ¼ x 25 ½

PLATE 92
Pigeon hawk
Falco columbarius
Merlin
Falco columbarius
25 ¾ x 20 ⅜

PLATE 93
Sea-side finch
Fringilla maritima
Seaside sparrow
Ammodramus maritimus
19 ¼ x 12 ¼

PLATE 94
Bay-winged bunting
Fringilla graminea
Vesper sparrow
Pooecetes gramineus
19 ½ x 12 ¼

PLATE 95
Blue-eyed yellow warbler
Sylvia æstiva
Yellow warbler
Dendroica petechia
19 ¾ x 12 ¼

PLATE 96
Columbia jay
Garrulus ultramarinus
Black-throated magpie-jay
Calocitta colliei
38 ⅛ x 25 ½

PLATE 97
Mottled owl
Strix asio
Eastern screech owl
Otus asio
25 ⅜ x 20 ¾

PLATE 98
Marsh wren
Troglodytes palustris
Marsh wren
Cistothorus palustris
19 ½ x 12 ¼

PLATE 99
Cow bunting
Icterus pecoris
Brown-headed cowbird
Molothrus ater
12 ¼ x 19 ⅜

PLATE 100
Green-blue, or white-bellied swallow
Hirundo bicolor
Tree swallow
Tachycineta bicolor
19 ⅜ x 12 ¼

PLATE CI
Raven
Corvus corax
Common raven
Corvus corax
38 ⅛ x 25 ⅜

PLATE CII
Blue jay
Corvus cristatus
Blue jay
Cyanocitta cristata
25 ½ x 20 ½

PLATE CIII
Canada warbler
Sylvia pardalina
Canada warbler
Wilsonia canadensis
19 ¼ x 12 ¼

PLATE CIV
Chipping sparrow
Fringilla socialis
Chipping sparrow
Spizella passerina
19 ½ x 12 ¼

PLATE CV
Red-breasted nuthatch
Sitta canadensis
Red-breasted nuthatch
Sitta canadensis
19 ⅜ x 12 ¼

PLATE CVI
Black vulture or carrion crow
Cathartes atratus
Black vulture
Coragyps atratus
25 ⅜ x 38 ¼

PLATE CVII
Canada jay
Corvus canadensis
Grey jay
Perisoreus canadensis
26 x 20 ¾

PLATE CVIII
Fox-coloured sparrow
Fringilla iliaca
Fox sparrow
Passerella iliaca
12 ¼ x 19 ½

PLATE CIX
Savannah finch
Fringilla savanna
Savannah sparrow
Passerculus sandwichensis
19 ⅜ x 12 ⅜

PLATE CX
Hooded warbler
Sylvia mitrata
Hooded warbler
Wilsonia citrina
19 ¾ x 12 ¼

PLATE CXI
Pileated woodpecker
Picus pileatus
Pileated woodpecker
Dryocopus pileatus
38 ¼ x 25 ⅝

PLATE CXII
Downy woodpecker
Picus pubescens
Downy woodpecker
Picoides pubescens
26 x 20 ⅞

PLATE CXIII
Blue-bird
Sylvia sialis
Eastern bluebird
Sialia sialis
19 ½ x 12 ⅜

PLATE CXIV
White-crowned sparrow
Fringilla leucophrys
White-crowned sparrow
Zonotrichia leucophrys
19 ½ x 12 ¼

PLATE CXV
Wood pewee
Muscicapa virens
Eastern wood pewee
Contopus virens
19 ½ x 12 ¼

PLATE CXVI
Ferruginous thrush
Turdus rufus
Brown thrasher
Toxostoma rufum
38 ¼ x 25 ⅝

PLATE CXVII
Mississippi kite
Falco plumbeus
Mississippi kite
Ictinia mississippiensis
25 ⅞ x 20 ⅞

PLATE CXVIII
Warbling flycatcher
Muscicapa gilva
Warbling vireo
Vireo gilvus
19 ⅜ x 12 ¼

PLATE CXIX
Yellow-throated vireo
Vireo flavifrons
Yellow-throated vireo
Vireo flavifrons
19 ½ x 12 ¼

PLATE CXX
Pewit flycatcher
Muscicapa fusca
Eastern phoebe
Sayornis phœbe
19 ½ x 12 ¼

PLATE CXXI
Snowy owl
Strix nyctea
Snowy owl
Bubo scandiacus
38 ¼ x 25 ⅝

PLATE CXXII
Blue grosbeak
Fringilla corulea
Blue grosbeak
Passerina cærulea
26 x 20 ⅞

PLATE CXXIII
Black and yellow warbler
Sylvia maculosa
Magnolia warbler
Dendroica magnolia
19 ⅝ x 12 ¼

PLATE CXXIV
Green black-capt flycatcher
Muscicapa pusilla
Wilson's warbler
Wilsonia pusilla
19 ⅜ x 12 ⅜

PLATE CXXV
Brown-headed nuthatch
Sitta pusilla
Brown-headed nuthatch
Sitta pusilla
19 ⅜ x 12 ⅜

PLATE CXXVI
White-headed eagle
Falco leucocephalus
Bald eagle
Haliæetus leucocephalus
38 ¼ x 25 ⅝

PLATE CXXVII
Rose-breasted grosbeak
Fringilla ludoviciana
Rose-breasted grosbeak
Pheucticus ludovicianus
25 ¾ x 20 ⅜

PLATE CXXVIII
Cat bird
Turdus felivox
Gray catbird
Dumetella carolinensis
19 ⅜ x 12 ⅜

PLATE CXXIX
Great crested flycatcher
Muscicapa crinite
Great crested flycatcher
Myiarchus crinitus
19 ½ x 12 ¼

PLATE CXXX
Yellow-winged sparrow
Fringilla passerina
Grasshopper sparrow
Ammodramus savannarum
19 ½ x 12 ¼

PLATE CXXXI
American robin
Turdus migratorius
American robin
Turdus migratorius
38 ¼ x 25 ⅝

PLATE CXXXII
Three-toed woodpecker
Picus tridactylus
Black-backed woodpecker
Picoides arcticus
26 x 20 ¾

PLATE CXXXIII
Black-poll warbler
Sylvia striata
Blackpoll warbler
Dendroica striata
19 ⅜ x 12 ⅜

PLATE CXXXIV
Hemlock warbler
Sylvia parus
Blackburnian warbler
Dendroica fusca
19 ½ x 12 ⅜

PLATE CXXXV
Blackburnian warbler
Sylvia blackburnia
Blackburnian warbler
Dendroica fusca
19 ¾ x 12 ¼

PLATE CXXXVI
Meadow lark
Sturnus ludovicianus
Eastern meadowlark
Sturnella magna
38 ¼ x 25 ⅝

PLATE CXXXVII
Yellow-breasted chat
Icteria viridis
Yellow-breasted chat
Icteria virens
25 ¾ x 20 ⅜

PLATE CXXXVIII
Connecticut warbler
Sylvia agilis
Connecticut warbler
Oporornis agilis
19 ½ x 12 ¼

PLATE CXXXIX
Field sparrow
Fringilla pusilla
Field sparrow
Spizella pusilla
19 ½ x 12 ¼

PLATE CXL
Pine creeping warbler
Sylvia pinus
Pine warbler
Dendroica pinus
19 ½ x 12 ⅜

PLATE CXLI
1
Goshawk
Falco palumbarius
Northern goshawk
Accipiter gentilis

2
Stanley hawk
Falco stanleii
Cooper's hawk
Accipiter cooperii
38 ¼ x 25 ⅝

PLATE CXLII
American sparrow hawk
Falco sparverius
American kestrel
Falco sparverius
26 x 20 ⅜

PLATE CXLIII
Golden-crowned thrush
Turdus aurocapillus
Ovenbird
Seiurus aurocapilla
19 ½ x 12 ¼

PLATE CXLIV
Small green crested flycatcher
Muscicapa acadica
Acadian flycatcher
Empidonax virescens
19 ⅜ x 12 ⅜

PLATE CXLV
Yellow red-poll warbler
Sylvia petechia
Palm warbler
Dendroica palmarum
19 ½ x 12 ⅜

PLATE CXLVI
Fish crow
Corvus ossifragus
Fish crow
Corvus ossifragus
38 ¼ x 25 ⅝

PLATE CXLVII
Night hawk
Caprimulgus virginianus
Common nighthawk
Chordeiles minor
26 x 20 ⅜

PLATE CXLVIII
Pine swamp warbler
Sylvia sphagnosa
Black-throated blue warbler
Dendroica cærulescens
19 ⅜ x 12 ¼

PLATE CXLIX
Sharp-tailed finch
Fringilla caudacuta
Saltmarsh sharp-tailed sparrow
Ammodramus caudacutus
19 ¾ x 12 ¼

PLATE CL
Red-eyed vireo
Vireo olivaceus
Red-eyed vireo
Vireo olivaceus
19 ½ x 12 ¼

PLATE CLI
Turkey buzzard
Cathartes atratus
Turkey-vulture
Cathartes aura
25 ⅝ x 38 ¼

PLATE CLII
White-breasted black-capped nuthatch
Sitta carolinensis
White-breasted nuthatch
Sitta carolinensis
26 x 20 ¾

PLATE CLIII
Yellow-crown warbler
Sylvia coronata
Yellow-rumped warbler
Dendroica coronata
19 ⅜ x 12 ⅜

PLATE CLIV
Tennessee warbler
Sylvia peregrina
Tennessee warbler
Vermivora peregrina
19 ⅜ x 12 ½

PLATE CLV
Black-throated blue warbler
Sylvia canadensis
Black-throated blue warbler
Dendroica cærulescens
19 ⅜ x 12 ⅜

PLATE CLVI
American crow
Corvus americanus
American crow
Corvus brachyrhynchos
38 ¼ x 25 ⅝

PLATE CLVII
Rusty grakle
Quiscalus ferrugineus
Rusty blackbird
Euphagus carolinus
25 ¾ x 20 ⅜

PLATE CLVIII
American swift
Cypselus pelasgus
Chimney swift
Chætura pelagica
19 ½ x 12 ⅜

PLATE CLIX
Cardinal grosbeak
Fringilla cardinalis
Northern cardinal
Cardinalis cardinalis
19 ⅜ x 12 ¼

PLATE CLX
Black-capped titmouse
Parus atricapillus
Carolina chickadee
Parus carolinensis
19 ½ x 12 ¼

PLATE CLXI
Brasilian caracara eagle
Polyborus vulgaris
Crested caracara
Caracara cheriway
38 ¼ x 25 ⅝

PLATE CLXII
Zenaida dove
Columba Zenaida
Zenaida dove
Zenaida aurita
25 ⅞ x 20 ¾

PLATE CLXIII
Palm warbler
Sylvia palmarum
Palm warbler
Dendroica palmarum
19 ½ x 12 ¼

PLATE CLXIV
Tawny thrush
Turdus wilsoni
Veery
Catharus fuscescens
19 ½ x 16 ½

PLATE CLXV
Bachmans finch
Fringilla bachmani
Bachman's sparrow
Aimophila æstivalis
19 ⅜ x 12 ⅜

PLATE CLXVI
Rough-legged falcon
Flaco lagopus
Rough-legged buzzard
Buteo lagopus
38 ¼ x 25 ⅝

PLATE CLXVII
Key-west dove
Columba montana
Key West quail-dove
Geotrygon chrysia
20 ⅞ x 25 ⅞

PLATE CLXVIII
Forked-tailed flycatcher
Muscicapa savana
Fork-tailed flycatcher
Tyrannus savana
19 ⅜ x 12 ¼

PLATE CLXIX
Mangrove cuckoo
Coccyzus seniculus
Mangrove cuckoo
Coccyzus minor
19 ½ x 12 ⅜

PLATE CLXX
Gray tyrant
Tyrannus grisens
Grey kingbird
Tyrannus dominicensis
19 ¾ x 12 ¼

PLATE CLXXI
Barn owl
Strix flammea
Barn owl
Tyto alba
38 ¼ x 25 ⅝

PLATE CLXXII
Blue-headed pigeon
Columba cyanocephala
Blue-headed quail-dove
Starnœnas cyanocephala
20 ⅞ x 26

PLATE CLXXIII
Barn swallow
Hirundo americana
Barn swallow
Hirundo rustica
19 ½ x 12 ¼

PLATE CLXXIV
Olive sided flycatcher
Muscicapa inornata
Olive-sided flycatcher
Contopus cooperi
19 ⅜ x 12 ¼

PLATE CLXXV
Nuttalls lesser-marsh wren
Troglodites brevirostris
Sedge wren
Cistothorus platensis
19 ½ x 12 ¼

PLATE CLXXVI
Spotted grous
Tetrao canadensis
Spruce grouse
Canachites canadensis
25 ½ x 38 ⅜

PLATE CLXXVII
White-crowned pigeon
Columba leucocephala
White-crowned pigeon
Columba leucocephala
25 ⅜ x 20 ¾

PLATE CLXXVIII
Orange-crowned warbler
Sylvia celata
Orange-crowned warbler
Vermivora celata
19 ⅜ x 12 ⅜

PLATE CLXXIX
Wood wren
Troglodytes americana
House wren
Troglodytes œdon
19 ½ x 12 ⅜

PLATE CLXXX
Pine finch
Fringilla pinus
Pine siskin
Carduelis pinus
19 ½ x 12 ¼

PLATE CLXXXI
Golden eagle
Aquila chrysætos
Golden eagle
Aquila chrysætos
37 ¼ x 25 ⅝

443

PLATE CLXXXII
Ground dove
Columba passerina
Common ground dove
Columbina passerina
25 ⅞ x 20 ⅞

PLATE CLXXXIII
Golden-crested wren
Regulus cristatus
Golden-crowned kinglet
Regulus satrapa
19 ½ x 12 ¼

PLATE CLXXXIV
Mangrove humming bird
Trochilus mango
Black-throated mango
Anthracothorax nigricollis
18 ⅜ x 13 ¾

PLATE CLXXXV
Bachman's warbler
Sylvia bachmanii
Bachman's warbler
Vermivora bachmanii
20 ½ x 14 ¾

PLATE CLXXXVI
Pinnated grous
Tetrao cupido
Greater prairie chicken
Tympanuchus cupido
25 ½ x 37 ¼

PLATE CLXXXVII
Boat-tailed grackle
Quiscalus major
Boat-tailed grackle
Quiscalus major
26 x 20 ⅞

PLATE CLXXXVIII
Tree sparrow
Fringilla canadensis
American tree sparrow
Spizella arborea
19 ½ x 12 ¼

PLATE CLXXXIX
Snow bunting
Emberiza nivalis
Snow bunting
Plectrophenax nivalis
19 ½ x 12 ⅜

PLATE CXC
Yellow bellied woodpecker
Picus varius
Yellow-bellied sapsucker
Sphyrapicus varius
19 ⅜ x 12 ⅜

PLATE CXCI
Willow grous or large ptarmigan
Tetrao saliceti
Willow grouse
Lagopus lagopus
25 ⅝ x 38 ¼

PLATE CXCII
Great American shrike or butcher bird
Lanius septentrionalis
Great grey shrike
Lanius excubitor
26 x 20 ¾

PLATE CXCIII
Lincoln finch
Fringilla lincolnii
Lincoln's sparrow
Melospiza lincolnii
19 ½ x 12 ½

PLATE CXCIV
Canadian titmouse
Parus hudsonicus
Boreal chickadee
Parus hudsonicus
19 ½ x 12 ⅜

PLATE CXCV
Ruby crowned wren
Regulus calendula
Ruby-crowned kinglet
Regulus calendula
19 ½ x 12 ½

PLATE CXCVI
Labrador falcon
Falco labradora
Gyrfalcon
Falco rusticolus
38 ¼ x 25 ⅝

PLATE CXCVII
American crossbill
Loxia curvirostra
Red crossbill
Loxia curvirostra
25 ⅞ x 20 ¾

PLATE CXCVIII
Brown headed worm eating warbler
Sylvia swainsonii
Swainson's warbler
Limnothlypis swainsonii
19 ⅜ x 12 ¼

PLATE CXCIX
Little owl
Strix acadica
Northern saw-whet owl
Aegolius acadicus
19 ⅜ x 12 ¼

PLATE CC
Shore lark
Alauda alpestris
Horned lark
Eremophila alpestris
12 ¼ x 19 ½

PLATE CCI
Canada goose
Anser canadensis
Canada goose
Branta canadensis
38 x 25 ½

PLATE CCII
Red-throated diver
Colymbus septentrionalis
Red-throated diver
Gavia stellata
20 ⅞ x 28 ⅜

PLATE CCIII
Fresh water marsh hen
Rallus elegans
King rail
Rallus elegans
12 ¾ x 19 ½

PLATE CCIV
Salt water marsh hen
Rallus crepitans
Clapper rail
Rallus longirostris
19 ½ x 14 ⅞

PLATE CCV
Virginia rail
Rallus virginianus
Virginia rail
Rallus limicola
14 ¾ x 20 ⅜

PLATE CCVI
Summer or wood duck
Anas sponsa
Wood duck
Aix sponsa
38 ⅛ x 25 ½

PLATE CCVII
Booby gannet
Sula fusca
Brown booby
Sula leucogaster
25 ¾ x 20 ½

PLATE CCVIII
Esquimaux curlew
Numenius borealis
Eskimo curlew
Numenius borealis
10 ¼ x 19 ½

PLATE CCIX
Wilson's plover
Charadrius wilsonius
Wilson's plover
Charadrius wilsonia
12 ⅛ x 19 ⅜

PLATE CCX
Least bittern
Ardea exilis
Least bittern
Ixobrychus exilis
12 ¼ x 19 ½

PLATE CCXI
Great blue heron
Ardea herodias
Great blue heron
Ardea herodias
38 ⅛ x 25 ½

PLATE CCXII
Common gull
Larus canus
Ring-billed gull
Larus delawarensis
20 ⅞ x 26

PLATE CCXIII
Puffin
Mormon arcticus
Atlantic puffin
Fratercula arctica
12 ¼ x 19 ½

PLATE CCXIV
Razor bill
Alca torda
Razorbill
Alca torda
12 ¼ x 19 ½

PLATE CCXV
Hyperborean phalarope
Phalaropus hyperboreus
Red-necked phalarope
Phalaropus lobatus
12 ¼ x 19 ½

PLATE CCXVI
Wood ibiss
Tantalus loculator
Wood stork
Mycteria americana
25 ½ x 38 ⅛

PLATE CCXVII
Louisiana heron
Ardea ludoviciana
Tricolored heron
Egretta tricolor
20 ¾ x 25 ⅞

PLATE CCXVIII
Foolish guillemot
Uria troile
Guillemot
Uria aalge
12 ¼ x 19 ½

PLATE CCXIX
Black guillemot
Uria grylle
Black guillemot
Cepphus grylle
17 ½ x 20 ⅜

PLATE CCXX
Piping plover
Charadrius melodus
Piping plover
Charadrius melodus
12 ¼ x 19 ½

PLATE CCXXI
Mallard duck
Anas boschas
Mallard
Anas platyrhynchos
25 ½ x 38 ⅛

PLATE CCXXII
White ibis
Ibis alba
White ibis
Eudocimus albus
20 ¾ x 25 ¾

PLATE CCXXIII
Pied oyster-catcher
Hæmatopus ostralegus
American oystercatcher
Hæmatopus palliatus
12 ¼ x 19 ⅜

PLATE CCXXIV
Kittiwake gull
Larus tridactylus
Black-legged kittiwake
Rissa tridactyla
12 ¼ x 19 ⅜

PLATE CCXXV
Kildeer plover
Charadrius vociferus
Killdeer
Charadrius vociferus
12 ¼ x 19 ⅜

PLATE CCXXVI
Hooping crane
Grus americana
Whooping crane
Grus americana
38 ⅛ x 25 ½

PLATE CCXXVII
Pin tailed duck
Anas acuta
Northern pintail
Anas acuta
20 ¾ x 25 ¾

PLATE CCXXVIII
American green winged teal
Anas carolinensis
Green-winged teal
Anas carolinensis
12 ¼ x 19 ⅜

PLATE CCXXIX
Scaup duck
Fuligula marila
Greater scaup
Aythya marila
12 ¼ x 19 ½

PLATE CCXXX
Ruddy plover
Tringa arenaria
Sanderling
Calidris alba
12 ¼ x 19 ⅜

PLATE CCXXXI
Long-billed curlew
Numenius longirostris
Long-billed curlew
Numenius americanus
25 ½ x 38 ⅛

PLATE CCXXXII
Hooded merganser
Mergus cucullatus
Hooded merganser
Lophodytes cucullatus
20 ⅞ x 26

PLATE CCXXXIII
Sora or rail
Rallus carolinus
Sora rail
Porzana carolina
12 ¼ x 19 ½

PLATE CCXXXIV
Tufted duck
Fuligula rufitorques
Ring-necked duck
Aythya collaris
13 ¾ x 17 ⅜

PLATE CCXXXV
Sooty tern
Sterna fuliginosa
Sooty tern
Sterna fuscata
12 ¼ x 19 ⅜

PLATE CCXXXVI
Night heron or qua bird
Ardea nycticorax
Black-crowned night heron
Nycticorax nycticorax
25 ½ x 38 ⅛

PLATE CCXXXVII
Great esquimaux curlew
Numenius hudsonicus
Whimbrel
Numenius phæopus
20 ⅝ x 25 ¾

PLATE CCXXXVIII
Great marbled godwit
Limosa fedoa
Marbled godwit
Limosa fedoa
13 ¼ x 20 ⅞

PLATE CCXXXIX
American coot
Fulica americana
American coot
Fulica americana
12 ¼ x 19 ¼

PLATE CCXL
Roseate tern
Sterna dougallii
Roseate tern
Sterna dougallii
19 ½ x 12 ¼

PLATE CCXLI
Black backed gull
Larus marinus
Great black-backed gull
Larus marinus
38 ⅛ x 25 ½

PLATE CCXLII
Snowy heron or white egret
Ardea candidissima
Snowy egret
Egretta thula
25 ¾ x 20 ½

PLATE CCXLIII
American snipe
Scolopax wilsonii
Common snipe
Gallinago gallinago
12 ¼ x 19 ⅜

PLATE CCXLIV
Common gallinule
Gallinula chloropus
Common moorhen
Gallinula chloropus
12 ¼ x 19 ⅜

PLATE CCXLV
[No common name given]
Uria brunnichii
Brunnich's guillemot
Uria lomvia
12 ¼ x 21 ½

PLATE CCXLVI
Eider duck
Fuligula mollissima
Common eider
Somateria mollissima
25 ½ x 38 ⅛

PLATE CCXLVII
Velvet duck
Fuligula fusca
Velvet scoter
Melanitta fusca
20 ⅝ x 29 ⅞

CCXLVIII
American pied-bill dobchick
Podiceps carolinensis
Pied-billed grebe
Podilymbus podiceps
14 ⅝ x 22 ¼

PLATE CCXLIX
Tufted auk
Mormon cirrhatus
Tufted puffin
Fratercula cirrhata
14 ¼ x 19 ½

PLATE CCL
Arctic tern
Sterna arctica
Arctic tern
Sterna paradisæa
19 ⅜ x 12 ¼

PLATE CCLI
Brown pelican
Pelecanus fuscus
Brown pelican
Pelecanus occidentalis
38 ⅛ x 25 ½

PLATE CCLII
Florida cormorant
Carbo floridanus
Double-crested cormorant
Phalacrocorax auritus
19 ¾ x 26 ⅛

PLATE CCLIII
Jager
Lestris pomarina
Pomarine skua
Stercorarius pomarinus
15 ¾ x 21 ¼

PLATE CCLVI
Wilson's phalarope
Phalaropus wilsonii
Wilson's phalarope
Phalaropus tricolor
15 ¾ x 21 ¼

PLATE CCLV
Red phalarope
Phalaropus platyrhynchus
Grey phalarope
Phalaropus fulicarius
15 ¾ x 22 ½

PLATE CCLVI
Purple heron
Ardea rufescens
Reddish egret
Egretta rufescens
25 ½ x 38 ¼

PLATE CCLVII
Double-crested cormorant
Phalacrocorax dilophus
Double-crested cormorant
Phalacrocorax auritus
30 ¼ x 21 ⅝

PLATE CCLVIII
Hudsonian godwit
Limosa hudsonica
Hudsonian godwit
Limosa hæmastica
14 ¾ x 20 ⅜

PLATE CCLIX
Horned grebe
Podiceps cornutus
Horned grebe
Podiceps auritus
14 ¾ x 20 ⅜

PLATE CCLX
Fork-tail petrel
Thalassidroma leachii
Leach's storm petrel
Oceanodroma leucorhoa
12 ¼ x 19 ⅜

PLATE CCLXI
Hooping crane
Grus americana
Sandhill crane
Grus canadensis
38 ⅛ x 25 ½

PLATE CCLXII
Tropic bird
Phæton æthereus
White-tailed tropicbird
Phæthon lepturus
20 ⅝ x 29 ⅞

PLATE CCLXIII
Pigmy curlew
Tringa subarquata
Curlew sandpiper
Calidris ferruginea
12 ⅛ x 19 ¼

PLATE CCLXIV
Fulmar petrel
Procellaria glacialis
Northern fulmar
Fulmarus glacialis
12 ¼ x 19 ⅜

PLATE CCLXV
Buff breasted sandpiper
Tringa rufescens
Buff-breasted sandpiper
Tryngites subruficollis
12 ¼ x 19 ⅜

PLATE CCLXVI
Common cormorant
Phalacrocorax carbo
Great cormorant
Phalacrocorax carbo
25 x 38 ⅛

PLATE CCLXVII
Arctic yager
Lestris parasitica
Long-tailed skua
Stercorarius longicaudus
30 x 21 ⅝

PLATE CCLXVIII
American woodcock
Scolopax minor
American woodcock
Scolopax minor
14 ⅝ x 20 ⅜

PLATE CCLXIX
Greenshank
Totanus glottis
Common greenshank
Tringa nebularia
14 ¾ x 20 ⅜

PLATE CCLXX
Stormy petrel
Thalassidroma wilsonii
Wilson's storm petrel
Oceanites oceanicus
12 ⅜ x 19 ½

PLATE CCLXXI
Frigate pelican
Tachypetes aquilus
Magnificent frigatebird
Fregata magnificens
38 ⅛ x 25 ½

PLATE CCLXXII
Richardson's jager
Lestris richardsonii
Arctic skua
Stercorarius parasiticus
20 ⅝ x 25 ¾

PLATE CCLXXIII
Cayenne tern
Sterna cayana
Royal tern
Sterna maxima
14 ⅞ x 20 ½

PLATE CCLXXIV
Semipalmated shipe or willet
Totanus semipalmatus
Willet
Catoptrophorus semipalmatus
14 ¾ x 20 ½

PLATE CCLXXV
Noddy tern
Sterna stolida
Brown noddy
Anous stolidus
12 ⅛ x 19 ¼

PLATE CCLXXVI
King duck
Fuligula spectabilis
King eider
Somateria spectabilis
25 ½ x 38 ⅛

PLATE CCLXXVII
Hutchins's barnacle goose
Anser hutchinsii
Canada goose
Branta canadensis
26 x 21 ⅞

PLATE CCLXXVIII
Schinz's sandpiper
Tringa schinzii
White-rumped sandpiper
Calidris fuscicollis
12 ⅛ x 19 ¼

PLATE CCLXXIX
Sandwich tern
Sterna boysii
Sandwich tern
Sterna sandvicensis
12 ⅛ x 19 ¼

PLATE CCLXXX
Black tern
Sterna nigra
Black tern
Childonias niger
19 ⅝ x 12 ⅜

PLATE CCLXXXI
Great white heron
Ardea occidentalis
Great blue heron
Ardea herodias
25 ½ x 38 ⅛

PLATE CCLXXXII
White-winged silvery gull
Larus leucopterus
Iceland gull
Larus glaucoides
20 ⅝ x 25 ⅞

PLATE CCLXXXIII
Wandering shearwater
Puffinus cinereus
Great shearwater
Puffinus gravis
12 ⅜ x 19 ⅜

PLATE CCLXXXIV
Purple sandpiper
Tringa maritima
Purple sandpiper
Calidris maritima
12 ⅜ x 19 ⅜

PLATE CCLXXXV
Fork-tailed gull
Larus sabini
Sabine's gull and sanderling
Xema sabini and *Calidris alba*
12 ¼ x 19 ¼

PLATE CCLXXXVI
White-fronted goose
Anser albifrons
Greater white-fronted goose
Anser albifrons
25 ½ x 38 ⅛

PLATE CCLXXXVII
Ivory gull
Larus eburneus
Ivory gull
Pagophila eburnea
20 ⅝ x 30 ⅛

PLATE CCLXXXVIII
Yellow shank
Totanus flavipes
Lesser yellowlegs
Tringa flavipes
14 ⅝ x 20 ¼

PLATE CCLXXXIX
Solitary sandpiper
Totanus chloropygius
Solitary sandpiper
Tringa solitaria
12 ¼ x 19 ¼

PLATE CCXC
Red backed sandpiper
Tringa alpina
Dunlin
Calidris alpina
12 ⅛ x 19 ⅜

PLATE CCXCI
Herring gull
Larus argentatus
Herring gull
Larus argentatus
38 ⅛ x 25 ½

PLATE CCXCII
Crested grebe
Podiceps cristatus
Great crested grebe
Podiceps cristatus
20 ⅝ x 30 ⅛

PLATE CCXCIII
Large billed puffin
Mormon glacialis
Horned puffin
Fratercula corniculata
14 ¾ x 20 ½

PLATE CCXCIV
Pectoral sandpiper
Tringa pectoralis
Pectoral sandpiper
Calidris melanotos
12 ⅛ x 19 ¼

PLATE CCXCV
Manks shearwater
Puffinus anglorum
Manx shearwater
Puffinus puffinus
12 ¼ x 19 ¼

PLATE CCXCVI
Barnacle goose
Anser leucopsis
Barnacle goose
Branta leucopsis
25 ½ x 38 ⅛

PLATE CCXCVII
Harlequin duck
Fuligula histrionica
Harlequin duck
Histrionicus histrionicus
20 ⅝ x 30 ¼

PLATE CCXCVIII
Red-necked grebe
Podiceps rubricollis
Red-necked grebe
Podiceps grisegena
14 ¾ x 20 ⅜

PLATE CCXCIX
Dusky petrel
Puffinus obscurus
Audubon's shearwater
Puffinus lherminieri
12 ¼ x 19 ⅜

PLATE CCC
Golden plover
Charadrius pluvialis
American golden plover
Pluvialis dominica
14 ¾ x 20 ½

PLATE CCCI
Canvas backed duck
Fuligula vallisneria
Canvasback
Aythya valisineria
25 ½ x 38 ⅛

PLATE CCCII
Dusky duck
Anas obscura
American black duck
Anas rubripes
21 ⅛ x 30 ⅜

PLATE CCCIII
Bartram sandpiper
Totanus bartramius
Upland sandpiper
Bartramia longicauda
14 ⅞ x 21

PLATE CCCIV
Turn-stone
Strepsilas interpres
Ruddy turnstone
Arenaria interpres
14 ¾ x 21 ⅝

PLATE CCCV
Purple gallinule
Gallinula martinica
American purple gallinule
Porphyrio martinica
12 ⅜ x 19 ½

PLATE CCCVI
Great northern diver or loon
Colymbus glacialis
Great northern diver
Gavia immer
25 ⅝ x 38 ¼

PLATE CCCVII
Blue crane or heron
Ardea cærulea
Little blue heron
Egretta cærulea
21 ¼ x 30 ½

PLATE CCCVIII
Tell-tale godwit or snipe
Totanus melanoleucus
Greater yellowlegs
Tringa melanoleuca
14 ⅞ x 21

PLATE CCCIX
Great tern
Sterna hirundo
Common tern
Sterna hirundo
19 ⅜ x 15 ¼

PLATE CCCX
Spotted sandpiper
Totanus macularius
Spotted sandpiper
Actitis macularius
14 ⅝ x 21 ⅛

PLATE CCCXI
American white pelican
Pelicanus americanus
American white pelican
Pelecanus erythrorhynchos
38 ¼ x 25 ¾

PLATE CCCXII
Long-tailed duck
Fuligula glacialis
Long-tailed duck
Clangula hyemalis
21 ¼ x 30 ¼

PLATE CCCXIII
Blue-winged teal
Anas discors
Blue-winged teal
Anas discors
14 ¾ x 20 ½

PLATE CCCXIV
Black-headed gull
Larus atricilla
Laughing gull
Larus atricilla
14 ¾ x 20 ½

PLATE CCCXV
Red-breasted sandpiper
Tringa islandica
Red knot
Calidris canutus
12 ¼ x 19 ½

PLATE CCCXVI
Black-bellied darter
Plotus anhinga
Anhinga
Anhinga anhinga
38 ¼ x 25 ⅝

PLATE CCCXVII
Black or surf duck
Fuligula perspicillata
Surf scoter
Melanitta perspicillata
21 ¼ x 30 ¼

PLATE CCCXVIII
American avocet
Recurvirostra americana
American avocet
Recurvirostra americana
14 ⅝ x 20 ⅜

PLATE CCCXIX
Lesser tern
Sterna minuta
Least tern
Sterna antillarum
19 ½ x 12 ¼

PLATE CCCXX
Little sandpiper
Tringa pusilla
Least sandpiper
Calidris minutilla
14 ¾ x 20 ½

PLATE CCCXXI
Roseate spoonbill
Platalea ajaja
Roseate spoonbill
Ajaia ajaja
25 ⅝ x 35 ¼

PLATE CCCXXII
Red-headed duck
Fuligula ferina
Redhead
Aythya americana
20 ⅝ x 26

PLATE CCCXXIII
Black skimmer or shearwater
Rhincops nigra
Black skimmer
Rynchops niger
21 x 21 ⅛

PLATE CCCXXIV
Bonapartian gull
Larus bonapartii
Bonaparte's gull
Larus philadelphia
21 ⅛ x 16 ⅞

PLATE CCCXXV
Buffel-headed duck
Fuligula albeola
Bufflehead
Bucephala albeola
14 ⅞ x 20 ½

PLATE CCCXXVI
Gannet
Sula bassana
Northern gannet
Morus bassanus
25 ⅝ x 38 ¼

PLATE CCCXXVII
Shoveller duck
Anas clypeata
Northern shoveler
Anas clypeata
21 x 30 ¼

PLATE CCCXXVIII
Long-legged avocet
Himantopus nigricollis
Black-winged stilt
Himantopus himantopus
14 ⅞ x 20 ½

PLATE CCCXXIX
Yellow-breasted rail
Rallus noveboracencis
Yellow rail
Coturnicops noveboracensis
12 ¼ x 19 ½

PLATE CCCXXX
Ring plover
Charadrius semipalmatus
Semipalmated plover
Charadrius semipalmatus
12 ¼ x 19 ½

PLATE CCCXXXI
Goosander
Mergus merganser
Goosander
Mergus merganser
25 ⅝ x 38 ¼

PLATE CCCXXXII
Pied duck
Fuligula labradora
Labrador duck
Camptorhynchus labradorius
21 ¼ x 30 ⅛

PLATE CCCXXXIII
Green heron
Ardea virescens
Green heron
Butorides virescens
20 ¼ x 22 ⅜

PLATE CCCXXXIV
Black-bellied plover
Charadrius helveticus
Grey plover
Pluvialis squatarola
15 ⅛ x 21

PLATE CCCXXXV
Red-breasted snipe
Scolopax grisea
Short-billed dowitcher
Limnodromus griseus
12 ¼ x 19 ⅜

PLATE CCCXXXVI
Yellow-crowned heron
Ardea violacea
Yellow-crowned night heron
Nyctanassa violacea
38 ¼ x 25 ⅝

PLATE CCCXXXVII
American bittern
Ardea minor
American bittern
Botaurus lentiginosus
22 ⅞ x 28 ⅛

PLATE CCCXXXVIII
Bemaculated duck
Anas glocitans
Mallard x gadwall
Anas platyrhynchos x Anas strepera
18 ½ x 23 ⅞

PLATE CCCXXXIX
Little auk
Uria alle
Little auk
Alle alle
12 ⅜ x 19 ⅞

PLATE CCCXL
Least stormy-petrel
Thalassidroma pelagica
European storm petrel
Hydrobates pelagicus
12 ½ x 19 ⅜

PLATE CCCXLI
Great auk
Alca impennis
Great auk
Pinguinus impennis
25 ⅝ x 38 ¼

PLATE CCCXLII
Golden-eye duck
Fuligula clangula
Common goldeneye
Bucephala clangula
21 ¼ x 30 ⅜

PLATE CCCXLIII
Ruddy duck
Fuligula rubida
Ruddy duck
Oxyura jamaicensis
16 x 26 ¼

PLATE CCCXLIV
Long-legged sandpiper
Tringa himantopus
Stilt-sandpiper
Calidris himantopus
12 ½ x 19 ⅞

PLATE CCCXLV
American widgeon
Anas americana
American wigeon
Anas americana
15 x 20

PLATE CCCXLVI
Black-throated diver
Colymbus arcticus
Black-throated diver
Gavia arctica
25 ⅝ x 38 ¼

PLATE CCCXLVII
Smew or white Nun
Mergus albellus
Smew
Mergus albellus
26 ⅜ x 22 ⅛

PLATE CCCXLVIII
Gadwall duck
Anas strepera
Gadwall
Anas strepera
16 ⅞ x 24 ⅞

PLATE CCCXLIX
Least water-hen
Rallus jamaicensis
Black rail
Laterallus jamaicensis
12 ¼ x 19 ½

PLATE CCCL
Rocky mountain plover
Charadrius montanus
Mountain plover
Charadrius montanus
12 ¼ x 19 ⅜

PLATE CCCLI
Great cinereous owl
Strix cinerea
Great grey owl
Strix nebulosa
38 ¼ x 25 ⅝

PLATE CCCLII
Black-winged hawk
Falco dispar
White-tailed kite
Elanus leucurus
30 ⅜ x 21 ¼

PLATE CCCLIII
1 and 2
Chesnut-backed titmouse
Parus rufescens
Bushtit
Psaltriparus minimus

3 and 4
Black-capt titmouse
Parus atricapillus
Black-capped chickadee
Parus atricapillus

5 and 6
Chesnut-crowned titmouse
Parus minimus
Chesnut-backed chickadee
Parus rufescens
19 ⅞ x 14 ½

PLATE CCCLIV
1 and 2
Louisiana tanager
Tanagra ludoviciana
Western tanager
Piranga ludoviciana

3 and 4
Scarlet tanager
Tanagra rubra
Scarlet tanager
Piranga olivacea
12 ⅜ x 19 ⅞

PLATE CCCLV
MacGillivray's finch
Fringilla macgillivraii
Seaside sparrow
Ammodramus maritimus
19 ½ x 12 ⅜

PLATE CCCLVI
Marsh hawk
Falco cyaneus
Hen harrier
Circus cyaneus
38 ¼ x 25 ⅝

PLATE CCCLVII
American magpie
Corvus pica
Black-billed magpie
Pica hudsonica
25 ½ x 21 ¼

PLATE CCCLVIII
Pine grosbeak
Pyrrhula enucleator
Pine grosbeak
Pinicola enucleator
20 ½ x 14 ¾

PLATE CCCLIX
1 and 2
Arkansaw flycatcher
Muscicapa verticalis
Western kingbird
Tyrannus verticalis

3
Swallow tailed flycatcher
Muscicapa forficata
Scissor-tailed flycatcher
Tyrannus forficatus

4 and 5
Says flycatcher
Muscicapa saya
Say's phœbe
Sayornis saya
21 ¾ x 14

PLATE CCCLX
1, 2 and 3
Winter wren
Sylvia troglodytes
Winter wren
Troglodytes troglodytes

4
Rock wren
Troglodytes obselata
Rock wren
Salpinctes obsoletus
19 ¾ x 12 ⅜

PLATE CCCLXI
Long-tailed or dusky grous
Tetrao obscurus
Blue grouse
Dendragapus obscurus
25 ⅝ x 38 ¼

PLATE CCCLXII
1
Yellow billed magpie
Corvus nutallii
Yellow-billed magpie
Pica nuttalli

2
Stellers jay
Corvus stellerii
Steller's jay
Cyanocitta stelleri

3
Ultramarine jay
Corvus ultramarinus
Western scrub jay
Aphelocoma californica

4 and 5
Clark's crow
Corvus columbianus
Clark's nutcracker
Nucifraga columbiana
26 ⅛ x 21 ⅞

PLATE CCCLXIII
Bohemian chatterer
Bombycilla garrula
Bohemian waxwing
Bombycilla garrulus
19 ¾ x 12 ½

PLATE CCCLXIV
White-winged crossbill
Loxia leucoptera
White-winged crossbill
Loxia leucoptera
19 ⅝ x 12 ⅜

PLATE CCCLXV
Lapland long-spur
Fringilla laponica
Lapland longspur
Calcarius lapponicus
12 ⅜ x 19 ⅝

PLATE CCCLXVI
Iceland or jer falcon
Falco islandicus
Gyrfalcon
Falco rusticolus
38 ¼ x 25 ⅝

PLATE CCCLXVII
Band-tailed pigeon
Columba fasciata
Band-tailed pigeon
Columba fasciata
29 ¼ x 21 ¾

PLATE CCCLXVIII
Rock grous
Tetrao rupestris
Rock ptarmigan
Lagopus muta
16 ¼ x 21 ⅜

PLATE CCCLXIX
1
Mountain mocking bird
Orpheus montanus
Sage thrasher
Oreoscoptes montanus

2
Varied thrush
Turdus nævius
Varied thrush
Ixoreus nævius
19 ¾ x 14 ½

PLATE CCCLXX
American water ouzel
Cinclus americanus
American dipper
Cinclus mexicanus
12 ⅜ x 19 ¾

PLATE CCCLXXI
Cock of the plains
Tetrao urophasianus
Greater sage grouse
Centrocercus urophasianus
25 ⅝ x 38 ¼

PLATE CCCLXXII
Common buzzard
Buteo vulgaris
Swainson's hawk
Buteo swainsoni
27 ⅜ x 23 ¾

PLATE CCCLXXIII
1
Evening grosbeak
Fringilla vespertina
Evening grosbeak
Coccothraustes vespertinus

2
Spotted grosbeak
Fringilla maculata
Black-headed grosbeak
Pheucticus melanocephalus
19 ½ x 12 ⅜

PLATE CCCLXXIV
Sharp-shinned hawk
Falco velox
Sharp-shinned hawk
Accipiter striatus
19 ½ x 14 ¾

PLATE CCCLXXV
Lesser red-poll
Fringilla linaria
Common redpoll
Carduelis flammea
19 ½ x 12 ⅜

PLATE CCCLXXVI
Trumpeter swan
Cygnus buccinator
Trumpeter swan
Cygnus buccinator
25 ⅝ x 38 ¼

PLATE CCCLXXVII
Scolopaceus courlan
Aramus scolopaceus
Limpkin
Aramus guarauna
21 x 33 ¼

PLATE CCCLXXVIII
Hawk owl
Strix funerea
Northern hawk-owl
Surnia ulula
26 ⅛ x 21 ⅝

PLATE CCCLXXIX
Ruff-necked humming-bird
Trochilus rufus
Rufous hummingbird
Selasphorus rufus
19 ⅝ x 12 ⅜

PLATE CCCLXXX
Tengmalm's owl
Strix tengmalmi
Tengmalm's owl
Aegolius funereus
20 ¾ x 15 ¾

PLATE CCCLXXXI
Snow goose
Anser hyperboreus
Snow goose
Anser cærulescens
25 ⅝ x 38 ¼

PLATE CCCLXXXII
Sharp-tailed grous
Tetrao phasianellus
Sharp-tailed grouse
Tympanuchus phasianellus
21 ⅝ x 29 ¼

PLATE CCCLXXXIII
Long-eared owl
Strix otus
Long-eared owl
Asio otus
19 ¾ x 12 ½

PLATE CCCLXXXIV
Black-throated bunting
Fringilla americana
Dickcissel
Spiza americana
19 ⅝ x 12 ⅜

PLATE CCCLXXXV
1
Bank swallow
Hirundo riparia
Collared sand martin
Riparia riparia

2
Violet-green swallow
Hirundo thalassinus
Violet-green swallow
Tachycineta thalassina
19 ⅛ x 15 ⅞

PLATE CCCLXXXVI
White heron
Ardea alba
Great egret
Ardea alba
25 ⅝ x 38 ¼

PLATE CCCLXXXVII
Glossy ibis
Ibis falcinellus
Glossy ibis
Plegadis falcinellus
21 ⅞ x 26 ⅛

PLATE CCCLXXXVIII
1
Nuttall's starling
Icterus tricolor
Tricoloured blackbird
Agelaius tricolor

2
Yellow-headed troopial
Icterus xanthocephalus
Yellow-headed blackbird
Xanthocephalus xanthocephalus

3
Bullock's oriole
Icterus bullockii
Bullock's oriole
Icterus bullockii
19 ¾ x 12 ⅜

PLATE CCCLXXXIX
Red-cockaded woodpecker
Picus querulus
Red-cockaded woodpecker
Picoides borealis
19 ¾ x 12 ¼

PLATE CCCXC
1
Lark finch
Fringilla grammaca
Lark-sparrow
Chondestes grammacus

2
Prairie finch
Fringilla bicolor
Lark-bunting
Calamospiza melanocorys

3
Brown song sparrow
Fringilla cinerea
Song sparrow
Melospiza melodia
19 ⅝ x 12 ¼

PLATE CCCXCI
Brant goose
Anser bernicla
Brent goose
Branta bernicla
25 ⅝ x 38 ¼

PLATE CCCXCII
Louisiana hawk
Buteo harrisi
Harris's hawk
Parabuteo unicinctus
21 ⅞ x 26

PLATE CCCXCIII
1
Townsend's warbler
Sylvia townsendi
Townsend's warbler
Dendroica townsendi

2
Arctic blue-bird
Sialia arctica
Mountain bluebird
Sialia currucoides

3
Western blue-bird
Sialia occidentalis
Western bluebird
Sialia mexicana
19 ½ x 12 ⅜

PLATE CCCXCIV
1
Chestnut-coloured finch
Plectrophanes ornata
Chestnut-collared longspur
Calcarius ornatus

2
Black-headed siskin
Fringilla magellanica
Hooded siskin
Carduelis magellanica

3
Black crown bunting
Emberiza atricapilla
Golden-crowned sparrow
Zonotrichia atricapilla

4
Arctic ground finch
Pipilo arctica
Spotted towhee
Pipilo maculatus
19 ⅝ x 12 ¼

PLATE CCCXCV
1
Audubon's warbler
Sylvia auduboni
Yellow-rumped warbler
Dendroica coronata

2
Hermit warbler
Sylvia occidentalis
Hermit warbler
Dendroica occidentalis

3
Black-throated gray warbler
Sylvia nigrescens
Black-throated grey warbler
Dendroica nigrescens
19 ⅝ x 12 ¼

PLATE CCCXCVI
Burgomaster gull
Larus glaucus
Glaucous gull
Larus hyperboreus
25 ⅝ x 38 ¼

PLATE CCCXCVII
Scarlet ibis
Ibis rubra
Scarlet ibis
Eudocimus ruber
21 ⅝ x 29 ⅜

PLATE CCCXCVIII
1
Lazuli finch
Fringilla amœna
Lazuli bunting
Passerina amœna

2
Clay-coloured finch
Fringilla pallida
Clay-coloured sparrow
Spizella pallida

3
Oregon snow finch
Fringilla oregona
Dark-eyed junco
Junco hyemalis
19 ½ x 12 ¼

PLATE CCCXCIX
1
Black-throated green warbler
Sylvia virens
Black-throated green warbler
Dendroica virens

2
Blackburnian warbler
Sylvia blackburniæ
Blackburnian warbler
Dendroica fusca

3
Mourning warbler
Sylvia philadelphia
MacGillivray's warbler
Oporornis tolmiei
19 ½ x 12 ¼

PLATE CCCC
1
Arkansaw siskin
Fringilla spaltria
Lesser goldfinch
Carduelis psaltria

2
Mealy red-poll
Linota borealis
Hoary redpoll
Carduelis hornemanni

3
Louisiana tanager
Tanagra ludoviciana
Western tanager
Piranga ludoviciana

4
Townsend's finch
Emberiza townsendi
Townsend's bunting
Emberiza townsendi

5
Buff-breasted finch
Emberiza picta
Smith's longspur
Calcarius pictus
20 x 12 ½

PLATE CCCCI
Red-breasted merganser
Mergus serrator
Red-breasted merganser
Mergus serrator
25 ⅝ x 38 ¼

PLATE CCCCII
1 and 2
Black-throated guillemot
Mergulus antiquus
1 Ancient murrelet and 2 Kittlitz's murrelet
1 *Synthliboramphus antiquus* and 2 *Brachyramphus brevirostris*

3
Nobbed-billed auk
Phaleris nodirostris
Least auklet
Aethia pusilla

4
Curled-crested auk
Phaleris superciliata
Crested auklet
Aethia cristatella

5
Horned-billed guillemot
Ceratorrhina occidentalis
Rhinoceros auklet
Cerorhinca monocerata
18 ⅝ x 28

PLATE CCCCIII
Golden-eye duck
Clangula vulgaris
Barrow's goldeneye
Bucephala islandica
12 ¼ x 19 ½

PLATE CCCCIV
Eared grebe
Podiceps auritus
Black-necked grebe
Podiceps nigricollis
12 ⅜ x 19 ⅝

PLATE CCCCV
Semipalmated sandpiper
Tringa semipalmata
Semipalmated sandpiper
Calidris pusilla
12 ⅜ x 19 ½

PLATE CCCCVI
Trumpeter swan
Cygnus buccinator
Trumpeter swan
Cygnus buccinator
25 ⅝ x 38 ¼

PLATE CCCCVII
Dusky albatros
Diomedea fusca
Sooty albatross
Phœbetria fusca
21 ⅝ x 28 ⅜

PLATE CCCCVIII
American scoter duck
Fuligula americana
Black scoter
Melanitta nigra
16 ⅝ x 21 ⅞

PLATE CCCCIX
1
Havell's tern
Sterna havelli
Forster's tern
Sterna forsteri

2
Trudeau's tern
Sterna trudeaui
Trudeau's tern
Sterna trudeaui
15 ¼ x 24 ¾

PLATE CCCCX
Marsh tern
Sterna anglica
Gull-billed tern
Sterna nilotica
19 ⅜ x 15 ⅞

PLATE CCCCXI
Common american swan
Cygnus americanus
Tundra swan
Cygnus columbianus
25 ⅝ x 38 ¼

PLATE CCCCXII
1
Townsend's cormorant
Phalacrocorax townsendi
Brandt's cormorant
Phalacrocorax penicillatus

2
Violet-green cormorant
Phalacrocorax resplendens
Pelagic cormorant
Phalacrocorax pelagicus
23 ¾ x 27 ½

PLATE CCCCXIII
Californian partridge
Perdix californica
Californian quail
Callipepla californica
12 ¼ x 19 ½

PLATE CCCCXIV
1
Golden-winged warbler
Sylvia chrysoptera
Golden-winged warbler
Vermivora chrysoptera

2
Cape may warbler
Sylvia maritima
Cape may warbler
Dendroica tigrina
19 ½ x 12 ¼

PLATE CCCCXV
1
Brown creeper
Certhia familiaris
American treecreeper
Certhia americana

2
Californian nuthatch
Sitta pygmea
Pygmy nuthatch
Sitta pygmæa
19 ½ x 12 ½

PLATE CCCCXVI
1 and 2
Hairy woodpecker
Picus villosus
Hairy woodpecker
Picoides villosus

3 and 4
Red-bellied woodpecker
Picus carolinus
Red-bellied woodpecker
Melanerpes carolinus

5 and 6
Red-shafted woodpecker
Picus mexicanus
Northern flicker
Colaptes auratus

7 and 8
Lewis' woodpecker
Picus torquatus
Lewis's woodpecker
Melanerpes lewis

9 and 10
Red-breasted woodpecker
Picus ruber
Red-breasted sapsucker
Sphyrapicus ruber
38 ¼ x 25 ⅝

PLATE CCCCXVII
1 and 2
Maria's woodpecker
Picus martini
Hairy woodpecker
Picoides villosus

3 and 4
Three-tœd woodpecker
Picus hirsitus
Three-tœd woodpecker
Picoides tridactylus

5 and 6
Phillips' woodpecker
Picus phillipsi
Hairy woodpecker
Picoides villosus

7
Canadian woodpecker
Picus canadensis
Hairy woodpecker
Picoides villosus

8 and 9
Harris's woodpecker
Picus harrisi
Hairy woodpecker
Picoides villosus

10
Audubon's woodpecker
Picus auduboni
Hairy woodpecker
Picoides villosus
30 ½ x 22 ½

PLATE CCCCXVIII
1
American ptarmigan
Tetrao mutus
Rock ptarmigan
Lagopus muta

2
White-tailed grous
Tetrao leucurus
White-tailed ptarmigan
Lagopus leucura
16 ¾ x 22 ⅞

PLATE CCCCXIX
1
Little tawny thrush
Turdus minor
Hermit thrush
Catharus guttatus

2
[No common name given]
Ptiliogony's townsendi
Townsend's solitaire
Myadestes townsendi

3
Canada jay
Corvus canadensis
Grey jay
Perisoreus canadensis
19 ½ x 12 ⅜

PLATE CCCCXX
Prairie starling
Icterus gubernator
Red-winged blackbird
Agelaius phœniceus
19 ⅜ x 12 ¼

PLATE CCCCXXI
Brown pelican
Pelicanus fuscus
Brown pelican
Pelecanus occidentalis
25 ⅝ x 38 ¼

PLATE CCCCXXII
Rough-legged falcon
Buteo lagopus
Rough-legged buzzard
Buteo lagopus
38 ¼ x 25 ⅝

PLATE CCCCXXIII
1
Thick-legged partridge
Perdix neoxenus
Crested bobwhite
Colinus cristatus

2
Plumed partridge
Perdix plumifera
Mountain quail
Oreortyx pictus
12 ¾ x 21 ⅜

PLATE CCCCXXIV
1
Lazuli finch
Fringilla amœna
Lazuli bunting
Passerina amœna

2
Crimson-necked bull-finch
Pyrrhula frontalis
House finch
Carpodacus mexicanus

3
Grey-crowned linnet
Linaria tephroncotis
Grey-crowned rosy finch
Leucosticte tephrocotis

4
Cow-pen bird
Icterus pecoris
Brown-headed cowbird
Molothrus ater

5
Evening grosbeak
Fringilla vespertina
Evening grosbeak
Coccothraustes vespertinus

6
Brown longspur
Plectrophanes townsendi
Fox sparrow
Passerella iliaca
20 x 13 ¼

PLATE CCCCXXV
Columbian humming bird
Trochilus anna
Anna's hummingbird
Calypte anna
19 ½ x 12 ¼

PLATE CCCCXXVI
Californian vulture
Cathartes californianus
Californian condor
Gymnogyps californianus
38 ¼ x 25 ⅝

PLATE CCCCXXVII
1
White-legged oyster-catcher
Hæmatopus bachmani
American black oyster-catcher
Hæmatopus bachmani

2
Slender-billed oyster-catcher
Hæmatopus townsendi
American black oyster-catcher
Hæmatopus bachmani
21 ¾ x 27 ¼

PLATE CCCCXXVIII
Townsend's sandpiper
Frinca townsendi
Surfbird
Aphriza virgata
18 ⅝ x 16 ⅛

PLATE CCCCXXIX
Western duck
Fuligula stelleri
Steller's eider
Polysticta stelleri
12 ¾ x 21 ⅜

PLATE CCCCXXX
Slender-billed guillemot
Uria townsendi
Marbled murrelet
Brachyramphus marmoratus
12 ¼ x 19 ⅛

PLATE CCCCXXXI
American flamingo
Phœnicopterus ruber
Greater flamingo
Phœnicopterus ruber
38 ¼ x 25 ⅝

PLATE CCCCXXXII
1
Burrowing owl
Strix cunicularia
Burrowing owl
Athene cunicularia

2
Large-headed burrowing owl
Strix californica
Burrowing owl
Athene cunicularia

3
Little night owl
Strix noctua
Little owl
Athene noctua

4 and 5
Columbian owl
Strix passerinoides
Northern pygmy owl
Glaucidium gnoma

6
Short-eared owl
Strix brachyotus
Short-eared owl
Asio flammeus
21 ¾ x 26

PLATE CCCCXXXIII
1
Bullock's oriole
Icterus bullocki
Bullock's oriole
Icterus bullockii

2
Baltimore oriole
Icterus baltimore
Baltimore oriole
Icterus galbula

3
Mexican goldfinch
Carduellis mexicanus
Lesser goldfinch
Carduelis psaltria

4
Varied thrush
Turdus nœvius
Varied thrush
Ixoreus nævius

5
Common water thrush
Turdus aquaticus
Northern waterthrush
Seiurus noveboracensis
20 ⅜ x 14 ⅛

PLATE CCCCXXXIV
1
Little tyrant fly-catcher
Tyrannula pusilla
Least flycatcher
Empidonax minimus

2
Small-headed fly-catcher
Muscicapa minuta
Small-headed flycatcher
Sylvania microcephala

3
Blue mountain warbler
Sylvia montana
Blue Mountain warbler
Sylvia montana

4
Bartram's vireo
Vireo bartrami
Red-eyed vireo
Vireo olivaceus

5
Short-legged pewee
Muscicapa phœbe
Western wood pewee
Contopus sordidulus

6
Rocky mountain fly-catcher
Tyrannula nigricans
Black phœbe
Sayornis nigricans
19 ½ x 12 ¼

PLATE CCCCXXXV
1
Columbian water ouzel
Cinclus townsendi
American dipper
Cinclus mexicanus

2
Arctic water ouzel
Cinclus mortoni
American dipper
Cinclus mexicanus
19 ½ x 12 ¼

Index

[Current common name and plate number]

Acadian flycatcher, plate CXLIV
American avocet, plate CCCXVIII
American bittern, plate CCCXXXVII
American black duck, plate CCCII
American black oyster-catcher, plate CCCCXXVII
American coot, plate CCXXXIX
American crow, plate CLVI
American dipper, plates CCCLXX, CCCCXXXV
American golden plover, plate CCC
American goldfinch, plate 33
American kestrel, plate CXLII
American oystercatcher, plate CCXXIII
American purple gallinule, plate CCCV
American redstart, plate 40
American robin, plate CXXXI
American treecreeper, plate CCCCXV
American tree sparrow, plate CLXXXVIII
American white pelican, plate CCCXI
American wigeon, plate CCCXLV
American woodcock, plate CCLXVIII
Anna's hummingbird, plate CCCCXXV
Ancient murrelet, plate CCCCII
Anhinga, plate CCCXVI
Arctic skua, plate CCLXXII
Arctic tern, plate CCL
Atlantic puffin, plate CCXIII
Audubon's shearwater, plate CCXCIX

Bachman's sparrow, plate CLXV
Bachman's warbler, plate CLXXXV
Bald eagle, plates 11, 31, CXXVI
Baltimore oriole, plates 12, CCCCXXXIII
Band-tailed pigeon, plate CCCLXVII
Barn owl, plate CLXXI
Barn swallow, plate CLXXIII
Barnacle goose, plate CCXCVI
Barred owl, plate 46
Barrow's goldeneye, plate CCCCIII
Bay-breasted warbler, plates 69, 88
Belted kingfisher, plate 77
Bewick's wren, plate 18
Black guillemot, plate CCXIX
Black phoebe, plate CCCCXXXIV
Black rail, plate CCCXLIX
Black scoter, plate CCCCVIII
Black skimmer, plate CCCXXIII
Black tern, plate CCLXXX
Black vulture, plate CVI
Black-and-white warbler, plate 90
Black-backed woodpecker, plate CXXXII
Black-billed cuckoo, plate 32
Black-billed magpie, plate CCCLVII
Blackburnian warbler, plates CCCXCIX, CXXXIV, CXXXV
Black-capped chickadee, plate CCCLIII
Black-crowned night heron, plate CCXXXVI
Black-headed grosbeak, plate CCCLXXIII
Black-legged kittiwake, plate CCXXIV
Black-necked grebe, plate CCCCIV

Blackpoll warbler, plate CXXXIII
Black-throated blue warbler, plates CLV, CXLVIII
Black-throated diver, plate CCCXLVI
Black-throated green warbler, plate CCCXCIX
Black-throated grey warbler, plate CCCXCV
Black-throated magpie-jay, plate 96
Black-throated mango, plate CLXXXIV
Black-winged stilt, plate CCCXXXVIII
Blue grosbeak, plate CXXII
Blue grouse, plate CCCLXI
Blue jay, plate CII
Blue mountain warbler, plate CCCCXXXIV
Blue-grey gnatcatcher, plate 84
Blue-headed quail-dove, plate CLXXII
Blue-headed vireo, plate 28
Blue-winged teal, plate CCCXIII
Blue-winged warbler, plate 20
Boat-tailed grackle, plate CLXXXVII
Bobolink, plate 54
Bohemian waxwing, plate CCCLXIII
Bonaparte's gull, plate CCCXXIV
Boreal chickadee, plate CXCIV
Brandt's cormorant, plate CCCCXII
Brent goose, plate CCCXCI
Broad-winged hawk, plate 91
Brown booby, plate CCVII
Brown noddy, plate CCLXXV
Brown pelican, plates CCLI, CCCCXXI
Brown thrasher, plate CXVI
Brown-headed cowbird, plates 99, CCCCXXIV
Brown-headed nuthatch, plate CXXV
Brünnich's guillemot, plate CCXLV
Buff-breasted sandpiper, plate CCLXV
Bufflehead, plate CCCXXV
Bullock's oriole, plates CCCLXXXVIII, CCCCXXXIII
Burrowing owl, plate CCCCXXXII
Bushtit, plate CCCLIII

Californian condor, plate CCCCXXVI
Californian quail, plate CCCCXIII
Canada goose, plates CCI, CCLXXVII
Canada warbler, plates V, CIII
Canvasback, plate CCCI
Cape may warbler, plate CCCCXIV
Carbonated warbler, plate 60
Carolina chickadee, plate CLX
Carolina parakeet, plate 26
Carolina wren, plate 78
Cedar waxwing, plate 43
Cerulean warbler, plates 48, 49
Chesnut-backed chickadee, plate CCCLIII
Chestnut-collared longspur, plate CCCXCIV
Chestnut-sided warbler, plate 59
Chimney swift, plate CLVIII
Chipping sparrow, plate CIV
Chuck-will's widow, plate 52
Clapper rail, plate CCIV

Clark's nutcracker, plate CCCLXII
Clay-coloured sparrow, plate CCCXCVIII
Cliff swallow, plate 68
Collared sand martin, plate CCCLXXXV
Common eider, plate CCXLVI
Common goldeneye, plate CCCXLII
Common grackle, plate VII
Common greenshank, plate CCLXIX
Common ground dove, plate CLXXXII
Common moorhen, plate CCXLIV
Common nighthawk, plate CXLVII
Common raven, plate CI
Common redpoll, plate CCCLXXV
Common snipe, plate CCXLIII
Common tern, plate CCCIX
Common yellowthroat, plates 23, 24
Connecticut warbler, plate CXXXVIII
Cooper's hawk, plates 36, CXLI
Crested auklet, plate CCCCII
Crested bobwhite, plate CCCCXXIII
Crested caracara, plate CLXI
Curlew sandpiper, plate CCLXIII
Cuvier's kinglet, plate 55

Dark-eyed junco, plates 13, CCCXCVIII
Dickcissel, plate CCCLXXXIV
Double-crested cormorant, plates CCLII, CCLVII
Downy woodpecker, plate CXII
Dunlin, plate CCXC

Eastern bluebird, plate CXIII
Eastern kingbird, plate 79
Eastern meadowlark, plate CXXXVI
Eastern phoebe, plate CXX
Eastern screech owl, plate 97
Eastern towhee, plate 29
Eastern wood pewee, plate CXV
Eskimo curlew, plate CCVIII
European storm petrel, plate CCCXL
Evening grosbeak, plates CCCLXXIII, CCCCXXIV

Field sparrow, plate CXXXIX
Fish crow, plate CXLVI
Florida scrub jay, plate 87
Fork-tailed flycatcher, plate CLXVIII
Forster's tern, plate CCCCIX
Fox sparrow, plates CVIII, CCCCXXIV

Gadwall, plate CCCXLVIII
Glaucous gull, plate CCCXCVI
Glossy ibis, plate CCCLXXXVII
Golden eagle, plate CLXXXI
Golden-crowned kinglet, plate CLXXXIII
Golden-crowned sparrow, plate CCCXCIV
Golden-winged warbler, plate CCCCXIV
Goosander, plate CCCXXXI
Grasshopper sparrow, plate CXXX
Gray catbird, plate CXXVIII
Great auk, plate CCCXLI

Great black-backed gull, plate CCXLI
Great blue heron, plates CCXI, CCLXXXI
Great cormorant, plate CCLXVI
Great crested flycatcher, plate CXXIX
Great crested grebe, plate CCXCII
Great egret, plate CCCLXXXVI
Great grey owl, plate CCCLI
Great grey shrike, plate CXCII
Great horned owl, plate 61
Great northern diver, plate CCCVI
Great shearwater, plate CCLXXXIII
Greater flamingo, plate CCCCXXXI
Greater prairie chicken, plate CLXXXVI
Greater sage grouse, plate CCCLXXI
Greater scaup, plate CCXXIX
Greater white-fronted goose, plate CCLXXXVI
Greater yellowlegs, plate CCCVIII
Green heron, plate CCCXXXIII
Green-winged teal, plate CCXXVIII
Grey jay, plates CVII, CCCCXIX
Grey kingbird, plate CLXX
Grey phalarope, plate CCLV
Grey plover, plate CCCXXXIV
Grey-crowned rosy finch, plate CCCCXXIV
Guillemot, plate CCXXVIII
Gull-billed tern, plate CCCCX
Gyrfalcon, plates CXCVI, CCCLXVI

Hairy woodpecker, plates CCCCXVI, CCCCXVII
Harlequin duck, plate CCXCVII
Harris's hawk, plate CCCXCII
Hen harrier, plate CCCLVI
Henslow's sparrow, plate 70
Hermit thrush, plates 58, CCCCXIX
Hermit warbler, plate CCCXCV
Herring gull, plate CCXCI
Hoary redpoll, plate CCCC
Hooded merganser, plate CCXXXII
Hooded siskin, plate CCXCIV
Hooded warbler, plates IX, CX
Horned grebe, plate CCLIX
Horned lark, plate CC
Horned puffin, plate CCXCIII
House finch, plate CCCCXXIV
House wren, plates 83, CLXXIX
Hudsonian godwit, plate CCLVIII

Iceland gull, plate CCLXXXII
Indigo bunting, plate 74
Ivory gull, plate CCLXXXVII
Ivory-billed woodpecker, plate 66

Kentucky warbler, plate 38
Key West quail-dove, plate CLXVII
Killdeer, plate CCXXV
King eider, plate CCLXXVI
King rail, plate CCIII
Kitthtz's murrelet, plate CCCCII

Labrador duck, plate CCCXXXII

Lapland longspur, plate CCCLXV

Lark-bunting, plate CCCXC

Lark-sparrow, plate CCCXC

Laughing gull, plate CCCXIV

Lazuli bunting, plates CCCXCVIII, CCCCXXIV

Leach's storm petrel, plate CCXL

Least auklet, plate CCCCII

Least bittern, plate CCX

Least flycatcher, plate CCCCXXXIV

Least sandpiper, plate CCCXX

Least tern, plate CCCXIX

Lesser goldfinch, plates CCCC, CCCCXXXIII

Lesser yellowlegs, plate CCLXXXVIII

Lewis's woodpecker, plate CCCCXVI

Limpkin, plate CCCLXXVII

Lincoln's sparrow, plate CXCIII

Little auk, plate CCCXXXIX

Little blue heron, plate CCCVII

Little owl, plate CCCCXXXII

Loggerhead shrike, plate 57

Long-billed curlew, plate CCXXXI

Long-eared owl, plate CCCLXXXIII

Long-tailed duck, plate CCCXII

Long-tailed skua, plate CCLXVII

Louisiana waterthrush, plate 19

MacGillivray's warbler, plate CCCXCIX

Magnificent frigatebird, plate CCLXXI

Magnolia warbler, plates 50, CXXIII

Mallard x gadwall, plate CCCXXXVIII

Mallard, plate CCXXI

Mangrove cuckoo, plate CLXIX

Manx shearwater, plate CCXCV

Marbled godwit, plate CCXXXVIII

Marbled murrelet, plate CCCCXX

Marsh wren, plate 98

Merlin, plates 75, 92

Mississippi kite, plate CXVII

Mountain bluebird, plate CCCXCIII

Mountain plover, plate CCCL

Mountain quail, plate CCCCXXIII

Mourning dove, plate 17

Nashville warbler, plate 89

Northern bobwhite (also red-shouldered hawk), plate 76

Northern cardinal, plate CLIX

Northern flicker, plates 37, CCCCXVI

Northern fulmar, plate CCLXIV

Northern gannet, plate CCCXXVI

Northern goshawk, plate CXLI

Northern hawk-owl, plate CCCLXXVIII

Northern mockingbird, plate 21

Northern parula, plate XV

Northern pygmy owl, plate CCCCXXXII

Northern pintail, plate CCXXVII

Northern saw-whet owl, plate CXCIX

Northern shoveler, plate CCCXXVII

Northern waterthrush, plate CCCCXXXIII

Olive-sided flycatcher, plate CLXXIV

Orange-crowned warbler, plate CLXXVIII

Orchard oriole, plate 42

Osprey, plate 81

Ovenbird, plate CXLIII

Painted bunting, plate 53

Palm warbler, plates CXLV, CLXIII

Passenger pigeon, plate 62

Pectoral sandpiper, plate CCXCIV

Pelagic cormorant, plate CCCCXII

Peregrine falcon, plate 16

Pied-billed grebe, plate CCXLVIII

Pileated woodpecker, plate CXI

Pine grosbeak, plate CCCLVIII

Pine siskin, plate CLXXX

Pine warbler, plate 30, CXL

Piping plover, plate CCXX

Pomarine skua, plate CCLIII

Prairie warbler, plate 14

Prothonotary warbler, plate III

Purple finch, plate IV

Purple martin, plate 22

Purple sandpiper, plate CCLXXXIV

Pygmy nuthatch, plate CCCCXV

Razorbill, plate CCXIV

Red crossbill, plate CXCVII

Red knot, plate CCCXV

Red-breasted nuthatch, plate CV

Red-cockaded woodpecker, plate CCCLXXXIX

Reddish egret, plate CCLVI

Red-bellied woodpecker, plate CCCCXVI

Red-breasted merganser, plate CCCCI

Red-breasted sapsucker, plate CCCCXVI

Red-eyed vireo, plates CL, CCCCXXXIV

Redhead, plate CCCXXII

Red-headed woodpecker, plate 27

Red-necked grebe, plate CCXCVIII

Red-necked phalarope, plate CCXV

Red-shouldered hawk, plates 56, 71

Red-tailed hawk, plates 51, 86

Red-throated diver, plate CCII

Red-winged blackbird, plate 67, CCCCXX

Rhinoceros auklet, plate CCCCII

Ring-billed gull, plate CCXII

Ring-necked duck, plate CCXXXIV

Rock ptarmigan, plates CCCLXVIII, CCCCXVIII

Rock wren, plate CCCLX

Roseate spoonbill, plate CCCXXI

Roseate tern, plate CCXL

Rose-breasted grosbeak, plate CXXVII

Rough-legged buzzard, plates CLXVI, CCCCXXII

Royal tern, plate CCLXXIII

Ruby-crowned kinglet, plate CXCV

Ruby-throated hummingbird, plate 47

Ruddy duck, plate CCCXLIII

Ruddy turnstone, plate CCCIV

Ruffed grouse, plate 41

Rufous hummingbird, plate CCCLXXIX

Rusty blackbird, plate CLVII

Sabine's gull and sanderling, plate CCLXXXV

Sage thrasher, plate CCCLXIX

Saltmarsh sharp-tailed sparrow, plate CXLIX

Sanderling, plate CCXXX

Sandhill crane, plate CCLXI

Sandwich tern, plate CCLXXIX

Savannah sparrow, plate CIX

Say's phœbe, plate CCCLIX

Scarlet ibis, plate CCCXCVII

Scarlet tanager, plate CCCLIV

Scissor-tailed flycatcher, plate CCCLIX

Seaside sparrow, plates 93, CCCLV

Sedge wren, plate CLXXV

Semipalmated plover, plate CCCXXX

Semipalmated sandpiper, plate CCCCV

Sharp-shinned hawk, plate CCCLXXIV

Sharp-tailed grouse, plate CCCLXXXII

Short-billed dowitcher, plate CCCXXXV

Short-eared owl, plate CCCCXXXII

Small-headed flycatcher, plate CCCCXXXIV

Smew, plate CCCXLVII

Smith's longspur, plate CCCC

Snow bunting, plate CLXXXIX

Snow goose, plate CCCLXXXI

Snowy egret, plate CCXLII

Snowy owl, plate CXXXI

Solitary sandpiper, plate CCLXXXIX

Song sparrow, plates 25, CCCXC

Sooty albatross, plate CCCCVII

Sooty tern, plate CCXXXV

Sora rail, plate CCXXXIII

Spotted sandpiper, plate CCCX

Spotted towhee, plate CCCXCIV

Spruce grouse, plate CLXXVI

Steller's eider, plate CCCCXXIX

Steller's jay, plate CCCLXII

Stilt-sandpiper, plate CCCXLIV

Summer tanager, plate 44

Surfbird, plate CCCCXXVIII

Surf scoter, plate CCCXVII

Swainson's hawk, plate CCCLXXII

Swainson's warbler, plate CXCVIII

Swallow-tailed kite, plate 72

Swamp sparrow, plate 64

Tengmalm's owl, plate CCCLXXX

Tennessee warbler, plate CLIV

Three-toed woodpecker, plate CCCCXVII

Townsend's bunting, plate CCCC

Townsend's solitaire, plate CCCCXIX

Townsend's warbler, plate CCCXCIII

Tree swallow, plate 100

Tricolored heron, plate CCXVII

Tricoloured blackbird, plate CCCLXXXVIII

Trudeau's tern, plate CCCCIX

Trumpeter swan, plates CCCLXXVI, CCCCVI

Tufted puffin, plate CCXLIX

Tufted titmouse, plate 39

Tundra swan, plate CCCCXI

Turkey-vulture, plate CLI

Upland sandpiper, plate CCCIII

Varied thrush, plates CCCLXIX, CCCCXXXIII

Veery, plate CLXIV

Velvet scoter, plate CCXLVII

Vesper sparrow, plate 94

Violet-green swallow, plate CCCLXXXV

Virginia rail, plate CCV

Warbling vireo, plate CXVIII

Water pipit, plates X, 80

Western bluebird, plate CCCXCIII

Western kingbird, plate CCCLIX

Western scrub jay, plate CCCLXII

Western tanager, plates CCCLIV, CCCC

Whimbrel, plate CCXXXVII

Whip-poor-will, plate 82

White ibis, plate CCXXII

White-breasted nuthatch, plate CLII

White-crowned pigeon, plate CLXXVII

White-crowned sparrow, plate CXIV

White-eyed vireo, plate 63

White-rumped sandpiper, plate CCLXXVIII

White-tailed kite, plate CCCLII

White-tailed ptarmigan, plate CCCCXVIII

White-tailed tropicbird, plate CCLXII

White-throated sparrow, plate VIII

White-winged crossbill, plate CCCLXIV

Whooping crane, plate CCXXXVI

Wild turkey, plates I, VI

Willet, plate CCLXXIV

Willow flycatcher, plate 45

Willow grouse, plate CXCI

Wilson's phalarope, plate CCLVI

Wilson's plover, plate CCIX

Wilson's storm petrel, plate CCLXX

Wilson's warbler, plate CXXIV

Winter wren, plate CCCLX

Wood duck, plate CCVI

Wood stork, plate CCXVI

Wood thrush, plate 73

Worm-eating warbler, plate 34

Yellow rail, plate CCCXXIX

Yellow warbler, plates 35, 65, 95

Yellow-bellied sapsucker, plate CXC

Yellow-billed cuckoo, plate II

Yellow-billed magpie, plate CCCLXII

Yellow-breasted chat, plate CXXXVII

Yellow-crowned night heron, plate CCCXXXVI

Yellow-headed blackbird, plate CCCLXXXVIII

Yellow-rumped warbler, plates CLIII, CCCXCV

Yellow-throated vireo, plate CXIX

Yellow-throated warbler, plate 85

Zenaida dove, plate CLXII